Vegetarian Times LOW-FAT & Fast
Asian

Also by the editors of Vegetarian Times *magazine*

Vegetarian Times Beginner's Guide (1996)

Vegetarian Times Vegetarian Entertaining (1996)

Vegetarian Times Low-Fat & Fast (1997)

Vegetarian Times Low-Fat & Fast Pasta (1997)

Vegetarian Times
Low-Fat & *Fast*
Asian

From the Editors of
Vegetarian Times magazine

Macmillan • USA

MACMILLAN

A Simon & Schuster Macmillan Company
1633 Broadway
New York, NY 10019-6785

Macmillan publishing books may be purchased for business or sales promotional use. For information please write: Special Markets Department, Macmillan Publishing USA, 1633 Broadway, New York, NY 10019.

Library of Congress Cataloging-in-Publication Data

Vegetarian times low-fat & fast Asian/by the editors of Vegetarian
Times magazine.
    p. cm.
   Includes index.
   ISBN: 0-02-861983-8
   1. Vegetarian cookery.   2. Cookery, Oriental.   3. Low-fat diet—
Recipes.   4. Quick and easy cookery.   I. Vegetarian times.
II. Title: Vegetarian times low-fat and fast Asian.   III. Title: Low-
fat & fast Asian.   IV. Title: Low-fat and fast Asian.
TX837.V4274   1997
641.5'636'095—DC21   97-30688
                                          CIP

Manufactured in the United States of America

10 9 8 7 6 5 4 3 2 1

Design by Amy Peppler Adams—designLab, Seattle

Contents

Acknowledgments

The Editors of *Vegetarian Times* want to thank everyone who assisted in the creation of this third volume in the Low-Fat & Fast cookbook series. Thanks first go to Hallie Harron, our recipe developer for this volume; her flair, unique style, and affinity for Southeast Asian cuisines shine in these recipes. Thanks also to Terry Christofferson, whose nutrition analyses and general hand-holding will always be remembered and appreciated.

And thanks to the staff at *Vegetarian Times* and at Macmillan, people too numerous to mention here, who made this all possible.

—Carol Wiley Lorente,
Special Projects Editor,
Vegetarian Times

Introduction

Welcome to *Vegetarian Times Low-Fat & Fast Asian*, the third in the series of cookbooks that are guaranteed to satisfy your need for healthful, meatless cooking and your desire to get food on the table fast.

Vegetarian Times has been the authority on meatless cooking and the vegetarian lifestyle since 1974. We first undertook the Low-Fat & Fast cookbook series in 1996 after the resounding success of our magazine *Low-Fat and Fast*. Based on our popular magazine column, it was named the Best Newsstand Introduction of the year. We knew the demand for low-fat recipes simply was not going to wane anytime soon.

And it hasn't. More than ever, Americans recognize that they need to eat a diet low in fat and high in complex carbohydrates to help prevent heart disease, obesity, diabetes, and the other illnesses that ravage our society.

But low-fat meals aren't enough. More and more Americans want meatless meals, they want them to taste good, and they want them quickly. That's what the Low-Fat & Fast cookbook series is all about. Each volume in the series offers 150 to 200 recipes—appetizers and snacks, main dishes, side dishes, and desserts. And whether you're a vegetarian for reasons of health, animal rights, environment, or religion, you'll find plenty to like here. All of the recipes are low in fat, take around thirty minutes to prepare, and call for few if any animal products (and no meat, fish, or poultry whatsoever).

HOW TO USE THIS COOKBOOK

The idea for a book of Asian recipes fits in seamlessly with the guidelines for a good diet: The Asian cuisines base their meals on complex carbohydrates, add lots of vegetables, and excel in the creative use of seasonings. Their diets also contain a healthful amount of soy foods, such as tofu, tempeh, and miso—foods that contain substances that have been shown to lower cholesterol and help prevent cancer.

vii

We've followed those guidelines here. Our recipe developer for this volume, Hallie Harron, is a caterer and restaurant consultant who spends part of every year in Southeast Asia, drinking in the culture and eating (and cooking) the food. An expert on the cuisines of China, Japan, Thailand, Malaysia, and Indonesia, she prides herself on the authenticity of her recipes. Yet they are simple to prepare. We are not kidding when we say that if you can boil water, chop vegetables, and stir, you can cook every recipe in this book!

We would encourage you to do a couple of things before you begin cooking. First, read "How to Cook Low Fat," "About Our Recipes," and "Stir-Fry Basics" below. Then take note of the glossary (page xiii). Whenever you come across an ingredient that is unfamiliar, refer to this glossary. Asian cooking will introduce you to ingredients you might not have tried before, but rest assured that you will be able to find them in any well-stocked supermarket, natural foods store, or Asian market. (Hallie developed and tested all of these recipes from her home kitchen in a very small town in rural Minnesota, and had no problems finding the ingredients!)

HOW TO COOK LOW FAT

Eating a low-fat diet and cooking low-fat meals isn't as difficult as you might think. Our advice has always been to base your meals and snacks on whole grains, beans, fruits, and vegetables; they're naturally low in fat and calories, and they contain all of the vitamins, minerals, and fiber you need.

Most of the recipes in this cookbook take around thirty minutes or less to prepare. But getting your own favorite meals on the table also can be easier when you know a few tricks. Most of it boils down to planning and completing tasks as the food cooks. Here are some tips for quick cooking:

- Set out all ingredients and utensils you'll need before you begin cooking, and mentally organize the preparation so you can "dovetail" steps. For example, while the rice is cooking, chop the garlic and ginger for the sauce. (We've written the recipes in this cookbook in such a manner to help you do this.) This is particularly important for stir-fries. (See "Stir-Fry Basics.")

- Organize and equip your kitchen to your advantage. Keep frequently used utensils, such as wooden spoons, rubber scrapers, spatulas, and whisks in a container or drawer next to the stove; keep pots, pans, mixing bowls, and measuring cups nearby. And return these items to the same places so you won't have to hunt for them next time.

- Wholesome, nutritious foods do come in convenient, prepared forms—use them! Frozen vegetables, canned beans, bagged, cut-up, and shredded produce, fresh noodles, canned vegetable broths, and other prepared foods are wholesome, of good quality, and save time. Don't forget the supermarket salad bar as a source for cut-up vegetables, and the canned food aisle for prepared garlic, ginger, roasted red peppers, and so on.

- There are simple ways to speed the actual heating and cooking of foods. Smaller and thinner cuts of vegetables cook more quickly than thick ones. Wide-diameter skillets and pots speed up heating and simmering. Also, when you need to boil water, start with hot tap water to speed things along. (Every little bit helps!)

ABOUT OUR RECIPES

After each recipe, we provide nutritional information that lists the amount of calories, protein, fat, carbohydrates, cholesterol, sodium, and fiber per serving. When a choice of ingredients is given (as in "skim milk or soy milk"), the analysis reflects the first ingredient listed (skim milk). When there is a range of servings (as in "1 to 2 tablespoons olive oil"), the analysis reflects the first number listed (1 tablespoon). When an ingredient is listed as optional, it is not included in the nutritional analysis.

We do not list the percentage of calories from fat per serving because we believe it is misleading. The percentage of fat in a given recipe is less important than the percentage of fat eaten in an entire day. The bulk of research indicates that fat intake must be less than 25 percent of calories to prevent disease and to promote health. So if you eat two thousand calories per day, you can eat fifty-five grams of fat per day and maintain a diet that obtains 25 percent of calories from fat.

Where appropriate, we also give variations and helpful hints after recipes.

STIR-FRY BASICS

A stir-fry is not only basic to Asian cuisine, but it's an American vegetarian standby as well—the perfect answer to that five o'clock question: What's for dinner? The following "recipe" for stir-fry should accommodate any kitchen pantry and can be adapted to include your favorite foods and flavors.

In order to get a stir-fried dish properly timed, make sure to have all ingredients ready before you start the process. If ingredients can be added at the same time, such as aromatics and liquids, mix them together before starting.

The following list includes the basic components of a stir-fry:

The Oil

Usually peanut oil or canola oil is the choice for a stir-fry; they are more healthful than the polyunsaturated oils (such as corn or soybean oil), have a high smoking point, and they do not provide any flavors of their own. Highly flavored oils, such as sesame or chili oil, usually pack too much flavor to be used on their own. Add a small amount of these flavored oils toward the end of the cooking.

The Aromatics

For any stir-fry dish, include minced or chopped garlic, minced fresh ginger-root, and minced chili peppers (any type).

For a Chinese dish, include scallions, fermented black beans, chili paste with garlic, red pepper flakes, and mung bean sprouts.

For a Japanese dish, include toasted sesame seeds, cubes of daikon radish, and wasabi.

For a Malaysian or Indonesian dish, include shallots and galangal.

For a Thai dish, include lemon grass, turmeric, Thai red or green curry paste, Thai keffir lime leaves, or minced or slivered hot green or red chili peppers.

The Vegetables

Broccoli florets, cauliflowerets, sliced carrots or celery, sliced fresh asparagus, julienned red or green bell peppers, sliced mushrooms, sliced green beans, sliced zucchini or summer squash, chopped or sliced onions, and so on.

The Protein (Optional)

Cubed tofu, tempeh, or seitan (also known as wheat gluten).

The Sauce

Liquids are added to provide more seasoning, to help steam the other ingredients in the dish, and to create a sauce that can be spooned over rice or noodles. (In this book, we have avoided thick, cornstarch-based blends in favor of lighter, broth-based, naturally thickened sauces.) Vegetable broth can form the base of most stir-fry sauces. Sauce ingredients also almost always include soy sauce, particularly in Chinese and Philippine dishes. Thai dishes will usually call for the addition of coconut milk (look for the low-fat varieties).

The Base

Cooked noodles or rice, plain or seasoned.

The Garnish

Fresh herbs have long been used in Asian and particularly Southeast Asian foods. Cilantro, basil, and mint are almost always welcome in Thai, Vietnamese, Burmese, and Malaysian dishes. Chinese dishes can often be garnished with cilantro; Japanese dishes with toasted and shredded nori (for instructions, see Helpful Hint, page 4). A good rule to follow: If the herb is used in the dish, use a sprig or two on top. Remember also that these sprigs, although called garnishes, are not meant to be like the Western ubiquitous piece of parsley; these sprigs add to the flavor, balance, and texture of the dish.

In addition, garnishing is one method of cutting fat in the dish. Since they are sprinkled on top, they hit the nose and palate first and seem stronger than they would if they were cooked into the dish. Therefore, you can use less of them and rely less on fat to carry the flavor of the dish.

To Prepare the Stir-Fry

Heat the oil in the wok until hot, just below the smoking point. Add the aromatics and stir-fry until fragrant, about 20 seconds, taking care not to burn them. (If they burn, discard them, wipe out the wok, and begin again. Burned aromatics will give the entire dish a burned taste.)

Begin adding the vegetables and protein, adding the firmer ones, such as tempeh and seitan, first. (Firm vegetables such as carrots, broccoli, cauliflower, and green beans can be lightly parboiled or steamed before preparing the stir-fry.) Stir-fry constantly, adding ingredients by the handful and stir-frying in between additions. Continue until all vegetables are added.

After 3 to 5 minutes of stir-frying (vegetables will be brightly colored and crisp), add the sauce ingredients. Stir-fry briefly to coat the vegetables with the liquid, and then cover the wok to steam the vegetables until they are just tender, about 2 minutes.

Serve over a base of noodles or rice and garnish.

ABOUT THE INGREDIENTS

Asian cuisine calls for ingredients that might be unfamiliar to the average American cook. Please take time to read the glossary (page xiii) to familiarize yourself with these ingredients, and refer to it whenever you come across a food that is new to you.

Most well-stocked supermarkets and natural foods stores have Asian food sections. Other Asian ingredients can be found in the produce section. And, of course, if you have an Asian market in your community, you're home free. Keep in mind that this cookbook was developed and tested in a home kitchen much like yours, located in a small community in the upper Midwest. All of the ingredients we call for in this book were readily available, so it is likely they'll be available where you live too.

We think you'll find *Vegetarian Times Low-Fat & Fast Asian* an invaluable guide to cooking fast, healthful, vegetarian meals. Happy cooking.

Glossary

All ingredients are available in supermarkets, natural foods stores, or Asian groceries.

Aburage   Also called yuba and bean curd sheets. A by-product of soy milk production, aburage is the skin that forms when soy milk cools after processing. Available frozen or dried in various shapes and sizes.

Asian apple pears   Also called Asian pears. Large, crisp, yellow fruits that look and taste like a cross between an apple and a pear.

Asian eggplant   Also called Japanese eggplant, these are identical in color and shape to regular eggplant, but much smaller.

Asian pears   See Asian apple pears.

Asian salad mix   A mixture of salad greens sold in packages in supermarket produce sections.

Asian sesame sauce   Sesame seed paste, similar to tahini but usually with added sesame oil.

Banana chili peppers   Long, yellow peppers so named because they resemble bananas in shape.

Bean curd sheets
See aburage.

Bean thread noodles   Also called cellophane noodles. Very thin, round, transparent noodles made from mung bean flour.

Black bean sauce   A prepared sauce made of pungent black beans and rice wine. Some varieties contain chili peppers and/or garlic.

Black sesame seeds   Similar to white sesame seeds, but slightly bitter.

Black vinegar   Vinegar made from rice, wheat, and millet or sorghum. Less tart but sweeter than regular distilled white vinegar. A good substitute is balsamic vinegar—just decrease the amount of sugar the recipe may call for.

Bok choy A cabbage with long white stalks and dark green leaves.

Brown bean sauce Also called ground brown bean sauce. A sauce made from fermented ground or whole soybeans. Some contain chili peppers.

Candied ginger See crystallized ginger.

Celery cabbage See Napa cabbage.

Cellophane noodles See bean thread noodles.

Chickpea flour A flour made from ground chickpeas (garbanzo beans).

Chili bean sauce Prepared sauce made of fermented soybeans and chili peppers.

Chili sauce Prepared sauce made of ground chili peppers and sometimes garlic, ginger, and other flavorings. There are many varieties. Thai chili sauce is sweeter than Chinese chili sauce, which is milder than the Vietnamese variety, so select according to taste.

Chinese chili sauce See chili sauce.

Chinese chives Available in spring and summer, Chinese chives can be green or yellow and are generally thicker than regular chives.

Chinese dried black mushrooms A general name for several varieties of dried mushrooms with brownish-black caps and tan undersides. Look for them in cellophane packages in produce sections.

Chinese five-spice powder Found in the spice aisle or Chinese food section, five-spice powder consists of ground Szechuan peppercorns, star anise, cinnamon, cloves, and fennel seed.

Chinese rice wine A wine made from fermented rice. Some examples are *Chia Fan* and *Hsiang Hsueh*.

Chunky fermented bean sauce A condiment and seasoning made from soybeans seasoned with wine, chili peppers, and salt.

Crystallized ginger Also called candied ginger. Ginger that has been cooked in syrup and coated with sugar.

Daikon radish Large, white Asian radish with a sweet, fresh flavor.

Dark soy sauce Soy sauce with the addition of molasses, which gives it a deeper flavor and darker color. Regular soy sauce can be substituted.

Duck sauce See plum sauce.

Enoki mushrooms Delicate, white mushrooms, sold in stalks of long white stems with tiny white caps.

Fermented bean curd
Fermented, seasoned cubes of tofu sold in jars. Available in two varieties: red, usually used in hearty dishes, and white, usually used in lighter dishes.

Fermented black beans
Fermented soybeans, used as a seasoning. They have a very salty flavor.

Galangal   Also called Thai ginger. The root of a ginger plant native to Southeast Asia, usually sold in powdered form and used as a seasoning.

Glutinous rice   See sticky rice.

Gomashio   Ground, toasted sesame seeds and sea salt used as a seasoning.

Ground brown bean sauce   See brown bean sauce.

Hoisin sauce   A popular Chinese condiment made of soybeans, garlic, chili peppers, and sometimes other seasonings.

Hot chili oil   Oil infused with hot chili peppers.

Japanese basil   See shiso.

Japanese eggplant   See Asian eggplant.

Jicama   Large, beet-shaped Mexican root vegetable with thin brown skin and crisp, white flesh. Can be eaten raw or cooked. The taste is between an apple and a pear, but not as sweet.

Kecap manis   Also called sweet soy sauce. A dark, thick, Indonesian soy sauce. For every tablespoon kecap, you can substitute one tablespoon soy sauce mixed with one teaspoon dark brown sugar.

Kim chee   Korean pickled cabbage used as a condiment. Extremely spicy.

Kombu   A wide, thick, dark green sea vegetable used as flavoring and usually discarded after cooking.

Lemon grass   An herb used throughout Southeast Asia. Resembles green onions, except it is woody and more yellow. Has a lemony flavor and aroma. Use only the tender, innermost part.

Lily buds   Also called tiger lily buds. Used as a vegetable and a garnish.

Lo mein noodles   Wide wheat Chinese noodles.

Lotus root   The root of the lotus flower. It has the texture of a potato and a flavor similar to coconut. Available canned or dried.

Lumpia   Philippine version of egg rolls.

Mai fun noodles   Very thin rice stick noodles.

Mandarin pancake   A thin, wheat pancake used in Chinese cuisine, especially in moo shu dishes. Sold in Asian markets and some grocery stores. Thin flour tortillas can be substituted.

Mild bean sauce   Same as chili bean sauce but with a milder flavor.

Mirin   A type of Japanese rice wine made from glutinous rice.

Mizuna   A crisp but feathery Japanese salad green. Usually available in mesclun and Asian salad mixes.

Mung beans
Tiny, greenish-brown beans, available in most supermarkets.

Mung bean sprouts
Sprouted mung beans, available fresh in the produce department and canned in the Chinese food section.

Napa cabbage   Also called celery cabbage. Football-shaped, light green cabbage with ruffled edges.

Nori   Thin sheets of seaweed usually used to wrap sushi. Available plain or toasted, although plain variety is usually toasted before using. Cut into thin strips, it is used as a garnish or seasoning.

Onion sprouts   Sprouted onion seeds used for flavoring.

Perilla   See shiso.

Pickled ginger   Gingerroot that has been pickled in sweet vinegar. Usually used as a condiment in Japanese cuisine.

Plum sauce   Also called duck sauce. A condiment, usually served in Chinese restaurants with duck, hence its name, that is made of plums, apricots, vinegar, yams, and spices. Each brand differs slightly in ingredients and flavor.

Preserved ginger
Gingerroot that has been preserved in a salt-sugar mixture. Usually used in desserts.

Radish sprouts   Sprouted radish seeds.

Ramen   Curly wheat noodles sold in brick form. Chuka soba is one variety.

Rice flour   A flour made from ground white rice. The glutinous or sweet variety is called *mochi* in Japan and is starchier. Used primarily as a thickener and occasionally in dessert baking.

Rice milk   A nondairy milk made from cooked rice.

Rice papers   A thin, edible paper made not from rice, but from a dough made with the pith of the rice-paper plant. Rice papers come in various sizes and are used like egg roll wrappers.

Rice vermicelli Thin, spaghetti-like, rice noodles.

Rice vinegar Vinegar made from fermented rice.

Rice wine Cooking wine made from rice. Some varieties are mirin and sake, which are Japanese rice wines, and Chinese rice wine.

Roasted chili paste A Thai seasoning and condiment made from roasted chili peppers.

Rose water Distilled rose petals used for seasoning.

Sake A popular alcoholic drink in Japan as well as a cooking wine used in sauces and marinades.

Sambal A condiment or side dish popular in Malaysian, Indonesian, and Sri Lankan cooking. Almost always contains chili peppers, brown sugar, and salt, although there are many variations that include other spices and herbs. Sambal oelek, your basic sambal, can be found in Indonesian and some Chinese markets.

Saté Also spelled satay. Saté is the Southeast Asian form of shish kebab—cubes of food, usually meat, on skewers, served with a spicy peanut sauce.

Seitan Also called wheat gluten. A chewy, meatlike, high-protein food made from boiled or baked wheat gluten. Available in dry mixes or prepared chilled in the deli section and prepared frozen.

Sesame oil The oil pressed from sesame seeds. Available in light and dark (also called "toasted") varieties. The dark variety has a stronger flavor. Sesame oil is generally used as a seasoning rather than as an oil for cooking because of its strong flavor.

Shiso Also called perilla and Japanese basil. A popular herb used in Japanese salads, sushi, and sashimi.

Shoyu Japanese soy sauce.

Soba Japanese buckwheat noodles.

Sticky rice Also known as glutinous rice and sweet rice. Very short grain white rice that becomes soft, moist, sweet, and sticky when cooked. Popular in savory dishes and desserts.

Straw mushrooms Dark brown mushrooms with long, dome-shaped caps. Usually available canned or in jars.

Sushi rolling mat A small, square, bamboo mat used to roll sushi.

Sushi vinegar A Japanese rice vinegar that usually contains sugar and sometimes other seasonings.

Sweet rice   See sticky rice.

Sweet rice flour   Flour made from glutinous or sweet rice, usually used in desserts.

Sweet rice wine   Some examples of the sweeter rice wines are mirin and *Chia Fan*.

Sweet soy sauce   See Kecap manis.

Szechuan peppercorns
The dried berries of an ash tree native to the Szechuan province in China. Available whole or powdered.

Tahini   Sesame seed paste with a thicker consistency than Asian sesame sauce.

Tamarind   A fruit similar to a date, widely grown in Asia, North Africa, and India. The pod contains seeds and a sweet-sour pulp that is dried and used as a flavoring in many foods. Available as syrup and in pulp form, canned paste, whole pods, or ground.

Tempeh   High-protein, cultured food made from fermented soybeans and sometimes grains. Sold in cakes, usually in the produce and frozen food section.

Thai chili sauce   See chili sauce.

Thai ginger   See galangal.

Thai curry paste   Sold in Asian markets and some supermarkets. Usually a blend of clarified butter, curry, vinegar, and other seasonings. Comes in red and green varieties. (See recipe for Thai Green Curry Paste, page 41.)

Thai keffir lime   A small, round, intensely flavored lime from Thailand. The leaves also are used as a seasoning.

Tiger lily buds   See lily buds.

Tree ear mushrooms
Fungus grown on trees. Usually sold dried, they resemble pieces of old, black leather.

Udon   Wide Chinese wheat noodles, usually available dried.

Umeboshi paste   A condiment made from Japanese sour plums that are salted, sun-dried, and aged. Contains enzymes believed to aid digestion.

Umeboshi plums   A variety of Japanese plums that have a sour taste. Available canned or in jars.

Vietnamese chili sauce   See chili sauce.

Wakame   A dark green or brown sea vegetable. The brown variety is more strongly flavored.

Wasabi   Japanese horseradish from the wasabi root. This fiery-hot horseradish is available as a paste, fresh root, and as a powder, which can be made into a paste by mixing it with water.

Water spinach   An Asian salad green whose flavor and

appearance resemble a cross between spinach and cress.

Wehani   An aromatic brown rice that resembles wild rice and has a sweet flavor.

Wheat gluten   See seitan.

White cabbage   A variety of common, round-headed cabbage.

White sesame seeds Regular, untoasted sesame seeds.

Wonton wrappers   Thin dough made from flour, water, and eggs. Available in several shapes and sizes, wonton wrappers are used to wrap fillings and to make dishes such as siu mai and potstickers.

Yuba   See aburage.

Yard-long green beans   Not quite a yard long, but their name is descriptive. These Chinese green beans are around twelve inches long.

Zest   The outer rind of citrus fruits, used as seasoning. Available dried in the spice aisle of the supermarket.

CHAPTER 1

Appetizers and Soups

Plum Barbecue Tofu Sticks

*These are sold by street vendors throughout China. Serve them as
part of a Chinese dinner or a summer Western barbecue.
(They can be prepared several hours in advance.)*

2 tablespoons plum sauce
2 tablespoons chili sauce
1 tablespoon hoisin sauce
¼ cup chopped scallions
1 teaspoon sesame oil
**14 ounces firm tofu, drained
    and cut into 1-inch cubes**
Twelve 6-inch bamboo skewers

Preheat the oven to 450°F.

In a medium bowl, mix together the plum sauce, chili sauce, hoisin sauce, scallions, and sesame oil. Skewer 4 or 5 cubes of tofu on each skewer and place on a nonstick or lightly oiled baking sheet. Brush them lightly with the sauce.

Bake the skewers until the glaze becomes shiny and slightly sticky, 10 to 12 minutes. Serve immediately with the rest of the sauce on the side.

Makes 12 skewers, 6 servings

Per Serving:
115 Calories; 11g Protein; 7g Fat;
6g Carbohydrates; 0 Cholesterol;
210mg Sodium; 2g Fiber.

Gingery Vegetable Congee

A congee is a rice-based side dish with a gruel-like consistency that is often served with various condiments such as soy sauce, sesame oil, hot chili sauce, or black bean sauce.

⅓ cup sticky rice plus ⅓ cup long-grain rice, or ⅔ cup long-grain rice
1½ teaspoons salt
6 cups water
1 tablespoon minced fresh gingerroot
1 small onion, thinly sliced (1 cup)
2 teaspoons minced garlic
1 medium bunch chopped scallions
2 cups vegetable broth

In a large saucepan or soup pot, bring rice, salt, and water to a rolling boil. Reduce heat and add the ginger, onion, and garlic. Cook, partially covered, for 1 hour, stirring occasionally so the rice does not stick to the pan. Add the scallions and broth. Heat for 5 minutes. Serve hot.

Makes 6 servings

VARIATION

Add 1 to 2 cups shredded bok choy, carrots, or napa cabbage, or snow peas with the ginger, onion, and garlic.

Per Serving:
89 Calories; 3g Protein; 1g Fat;
19g Carbohydrates; 0 Cholesterol;
917mg Sodium; 1g Fiber.

Daikon Sticks

This Japanese condiment, made from daikon radish, is actually more like a pickle. The flavor will intensify if stored in the refrigerator for several days.

**One 7-inch square nori, toasted
     (see Helpful Hint)
1 large daikon radish (about
     1¼ pounds), cut into
     1¼ × 3-inch sticks
2 tablespoons rice vinegar
1 tablespoon gomashio, or
     1 teaspoon salt plus
     2 teaspoons black
     sesame seeds
2 tablespoons soy sauce
1 teaspoon black pepper
1 teaspoon sesame oil
2 medium scallions, chopped**

Using scissors or a sharp knife, cut the toasted nori into ⅛ × 2-inch strips. Set aside.

In a large bowl, mix all of the remaining ingredients except the scallions. Just before serving, fold in the nori strips, leaving a few on top. Scatter the scallions over the top of the dish.

Makes 6 servings

Helpful Hint

To toast nori, hold the square over a medium-high flame for a few seconds, waving it back and forth. Alternatively, place nori square under a hot broiler, turning after 2 seconds. Be careful not to burn the nori.

Per Serving:
85 Calories; 6g Protein; 2g Fat;
12g Carbohydrates; 0 Cholesterol;
1,011mg Sodium; 7g Fiber.

Cold Sesame-Soy Eggplant

This may take a little longer than 30 minutes, but you won't be sorry!

**1 medium eggplant (1 pound),
sliced in half lengthwise**
1 tablespoon minced gingerroot
2 teaspoons minced garlic
1 teaspoon salt
3 tablespoons cilantro leaves
7 scallions (1 medium bunch)
1 tablespoon soy sauce
**1 tablespoon black or balsamic
vinegar**
½ to 1 teaspoon hot chili oil
**Croutons, bread rounds, rice
crackers, or raw vegetable
spears**

Preheat oven to 350°F.

Place eggplant cut-side down on a lightly oiled baking sheet or a nonstick baking pan. Bake until very soft, 45 to 50 minutes.

While the eggplant is baking, mix together the ginger, garlic, and salt and set aside on one part of the cutting board.

Mince the cilantro and scallion tops together. Set aside on another area of the cutting board. Chop the white part of the scallions and set aside in a small bowl. In a separate small bowl, mix together the soy sauce, vinegar, and chili oil. Set aside.

When the eggplant is done, let sit until cool enough to handle, then scoop out the flesh with a spoon or with your hands and place it in the center of the cutting board; discard the skin. Mash in the ginger, garlic, and salt, turning the mixture with a knife or scraper to mix it well. Mix in the cilantro and scallion greens, then pour the soy sauce mixture over the eggplant mixture and mix it well.

Transfer mixture to a serving bowl and top with the remaining chopped scallions. Serve immediately, or cover and refrigerate for up to 2 days before serving. To serve, spread the puree onto croutons, bread rounds or rice crackers, or use as a dip for raw vegetables.

**Makes a generous 1¼ cups,
about 6 servings**

Per Serving:
35 Calories; 1g Protein; 1g Fat;
7g Carbohydrates; 0 Cholesterol;
675mg Sodium; 3g Fiber.

Summer Sesame Egg Drop Soup

Here's a vegetarian egg drop soup that takes only minutes to prepare.

6 cups vegetable broth
1 egg plus 1 egg white, lightly
   beaten
1 teaspoon sesame oil
½ cup chopped scallions
Soy sauce

In a medium saucepan, bring the broth to a lively boil. In a small bowl, mix the eggs with the sesame oil. Pour the egg mixture in a thin stream into the bubbling broth, stirring constantly with a fork to form egg "threads." When the egg threads have formed, remove the pan from the heat and stir in the scallions. Serve the soup with a small pitcher of soy sauce on the side.

Makes 6 servings

Per Serving:
44 Calories; 4g Protein; 3g Fat; 4g Carbohydrates; 35mg Cholesterol; 1,020mg Sodium; 0g Fiber.

Eggplant and Tempeh Saté with Mint Sambal

*Saté is an Indonesian dish that usually features meat, fish, or poultry
on a skewer, and is served with a peanut sauce; sambal is a condiment that
usually contains chili peppers, brown sugar, and salt. Here's a
meatless saté, served with a mint sambal.*

**2 medium Asian (Japanese)
eggplants (about 8 ounces),
sliced ¼ inch thick
4 ounces regular or multigrain
tempeh, cut into ½-inch
cubes
1 recipe Mint Sambal (page 8),
prepared in a large bowl
Eight 8-inch bamboo skewers**

Preheat the oven to 450°F.

To soften the eggplant, place
the eggplant slices in a large bowl.
Pour boiling water to cover the
slices and set aside for 15 minutes.

Fold the tempeh into the bowl
of Mint Sambal. Drain the eggplant and add it to the bowl with
the tempeh; stir to coat the
eggplant slices. Thread the
eggplant slices and tempeh onto
the skewers, using 2 to 3 pieces of
each on every skewer.

Place skewers on a lightly oiled
or nonstick baking pan. Pour half
of the sambal mixture over the
skewers. Bake until the sambal has
lightly charred and the eggplant is
fully cooked, 15 to 20 minutes.
Serve hot with the remaining mint
sambal on the side.

**Makes 8 skewers,
about 4 servings**

Per Serving:
130 Calories; 7g Protein; 6g Fat;
14g Carbohydrates; 0 Cholesterol;
268mg Sodium; 4g Fiber.

Mint Sambal

2 tablespoons minced fresh
   mint leaves
1 medium shallot, chopped
   (about ¼ cup)
1 small hot green chili, seeded
   and finely minced
2 tablespoons lime juice
2 tablespoons unsweetened
   coconut chips or shreds
2 teaspoons canola or
   vegetable oil
1 cup finely chopped fresh
   pineapple
1 tablespoon soy sauce

In a large bowl, mix together all of
the ingredients.

Makes 1½ cups

Per Serving:
58 Calories; 1g Protein; 3g Fat;
8g Carbohydrates; 0 Cholesterol;
316mg Sodium; 1g Fiber.

Mushroom and Black Bean Wontons

*These are usually made with meat, but the chopped mushrooms
give an authentic flavor and texture.*

⅓ cup chopped water chestnuts
4 ounces firm tofu
8 ounces stemmed and
**   roughly chopped**
**   button mushrooms**
¾ cup chopped scallions
1 tablespoon black bean sauce
**   with garlic**
8 ounces thin wonton wrappers
1 tablespoon canola or
**   vegetable oil**
Hoisin sauce (optional)

In a food processor, mince together the water chestnuts, tofu, mushrooms, and scallions. The mixture should be slightly chunky. Transfer the mixture to a medium bowl and fold in the black bean sauce.

Assemble the wontons: Keep a small cup of water handy as you are filling the wontons. With your finger, moisten the edges of a wonton wrapper with a little water. Place 2 teaspoons of filling in the center of the wrapper. Fold the wonton to form a triangle. Then bring the two opposite corners of the triangle together to form a wonton. Place on a plate or parchment-lined baking sheet. Continue until you have used all of the wrappers and filling.

In a 10-inch nonstick skillet, heat 1 teaspoon of the oil over medium heat. Add 8 to 10 wontons at a time, taking care that they do not touch each other. Fry until the wontons are golden brown, 3 to 4 minutes on each side, reducing the heat if the pan begins to smoke. Repeat until all wontons are fried. Serve immediately. Serve with hoisin sauce if desired (hoisin sauce is a traditional accompaniment).

**Makes 30 wontons,
about 6 servings**

Per Serving:
175 Calories; 8g Protein; 5g Fat; 26g Carbohydrates; 3mg Cholesterol; 223mg Sodium; 2g Fiber.

Roasted or Grilled Shiitake Mushrooms

**2 tightly packed teaspoons
cilantro leaves**
2 teaspoons fresh gingerroot
**½ to ¾ teaspoon chili bean
sauce with garlic, or
to taste**
3 tablespoons vegetable broth
1 tablespoon dark soy sauce
**2 teaspoons canola or
vegetable oil**
**8 ounces fresh shiitake
mushrooms, cleaned
and stemmed**
2 teaspoons sesame oil

If roasting the mushrooms, preheat the oven to 350°F. If grilling, preheat the grill until the coals are gray to white.

Mince together the cilantro and ginger. Transfer to a small bowl and mix together with the chili bean sauce, broth, soy sauce, and oil. Rub each mushroom with the soy sauce mixture and place in a nonstick or lightly oiled baking pan. Place the pan on the grill or in the oven and cook until the mushrooms are soft and pliable, about 8 minutes. Drizzle the mushrooms with the sesame oil, and serve immediately.

Makes 4 servings

Per Serving:
75 Calories; 1g Protein; 5g Fat;
9g Carbohydrates; 0 Cholesterol;
307 mg Sodium; 1g Fiber.

Hot and Sour Soup

The classic Chinese soup.

5 cups vegetable broth
⅓ cup lily buds, soaked in 1 cup hot water for 20 minutes (optional)
6 Chinese dried black mushrooms (½ ounce), soaked in hot water for 20 minutes
1 tablespoon chopped tree ear mushrooms, soaked in 1 cup hot water for 20 minutes
2 tablespoons distilled white vinegar
1 tablespoon soy sauce
2 teaspoons sesame oil
1 teaspoon hot chili oil
Pinch of cayenne pepper
1 tablespoon cornstarch
1 tablespoon minced fresh gingerroot
2 teaspoons minced garlic
½ cup sliced bamboo shoots
½ cup firm tofu, cut into ½-inch cubes
1 large egg, lightly beaten
6 tablespoons chopped scallions (white parts only)

In a medium saucepan, heat the broth over medium heat. If desired, drain the lily buds; squeeze to remove any excess water; cut into strips; and set aside. Discard the soaking water.

Remove the Chinese mushrooms from the soaking water; squeeze to remove excess water; remove and discard the woody stems; and cut the mushrooms into thin slices. Strain the mushroom-soaking liquid and set aside 3 tablespoons. Remove the soaked tree ears from the soaking water; squeeze to remove excess water. Remove and discard any tough knobs. Cut the mushrooms into thin strips; discard soaking water.

In a small bowl, mix together the vinegar, soy sauce, oils, cayenne, cornstarch, and the reserved mushroom liquid; set aside. When the broth is at a simmer, stir in the ginger and garlic. Cook for 1 minute, then add the bamboo shoots, lily buds if desired, mushrooms, and tree ears. Cook for 3 minutes. Then stir in the vinegar-soy mixture and return to a boil. Cook for 30 seconds.

Remove from the heat and add the tofu cubes and beaten egg, stirring to blend the egg quickly and thoroughly. Serve in small bowls. Sprinkle with the scallions.

Makes 6 servings

Per Serving:
86 Calories; 5g Protein; 5g Fat; 7g Carbohydrates; 35mg Cholesterol; 1,032mg Sodium; 1g Fiber.

Indonesian Spicy Potato Sticks

A traditional tea-time snack.

1 medium shallot, minced
2 teaspoons minced garlic
2 teaspoons minced fresh
  gingerroot
1 hot green chili, seeded and
  minced
2 teaspoons canola or
  vegetable oil
2 tablespoons kecap manis or
  dark or regular soy sauce
¼ cup coconut milk
1 pound red potatoes, cut into
  3 × ¼-inch matchsticks
¼ cup chopped scallions
Spicy Tomato Sambal (page 54),
  optional

Preheat the oven to 400°F.

Oil a large baking sheet or line it with parchment paper.

In a blender or a food processor, puree the shallot, garlic, ginger, and chili into a thick paste. In a large wok or skillet, heat the oil over medium-high heat. Stir-fry the paste until fragrant, about 30 seconds. Add the kecap manis and coconut milk. Cook for 1 minute more. (There should be about ½ cup of very thick sauce.)

Add the potato sticks and toss with two spoons to coat the potatoes thoroughly. Spread them in one layer on the prepared baking sheet and bake until the potatoes are tender, 30 to 35 minutes. Turn on the broiler and broil the potatoes until they are crisp and lightly charred, about 2 minutes. (The potatoes should be a deep mahogany color and slightly sticky to the touch.)

Transfer the potatoes to a bowl and sprinkle with the chopped scallions. Serve immediately with sambal if desired.

Makes 6 servings

Per Serving:
126 Calories; 2g Protein; 4g Fat;
21g Carbohydrates; 0 Cholesterol;
361mg Sodium; 2g Fiber.

Miso Soup with Daikon, Tofu, and Asian Cabbage

Many Asians start the day with miso soup. It comes in hundreds of varieties and is a good source of nourishing soy protein.

6 cups water (see Helpful Hint)
One 3-inch strip kombu
About ½ daikon radish, peeled and grated (¾ cup)
1 cup shredded napa cabbage
¼ cup miso
1 cup drained firm tofu, cut into ½-inch cubes
½ cup chopped scallions
Soy sauce to taste

In a large saucepan, bring the water and kombu to a simmer. Simmer for 5 minutes, then remove the kombu and discard. Add the daikon and cabbage, and simmer until the cabbage is wilted, about 3 minutes.

Remove about ½ cup of the broth to a cup, add the miso, and stir into a smooth, thin paste. Pour the paste back into the soup along with the tofu cubes. Bring back to a simmer. Remove from the heat and pour into bowls. Sprinkle with scallions before serving. Soy sauce may be passed at the table if desired.

Makes 6 servings

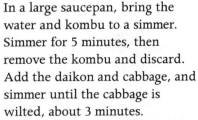

Helpful Hint

Do not substitute commercial vegetable broth for the water and kombu or the soup will be too salty.

Per Serving:
41 Calories; 3g Protein; 1g Fat; 5g Carbohydrates; 0 Cholesterol; 429mg Sodium; 1g Fiber.

Sweet and Hot Mung Noodle Cups

1 medium head Boston or butterhead lettuce
Two 2-ounce packages bean thread noodles
1½ tablespoons black bean sauce with garlic
1 teaspoon minced tangerine or orange rind
2 tablespoons tangerine or orange juice
2 tablespoons rice wine
⅓ cup chopped scallions
2 tangerines or 1 medium orange, peeled, seeded, sectioned, and chopped (¾ cup)

Place 6 of the biggest unblemished lettuce leaves on a serving platter.

Place the dried noodles in a medium bowl. Pour boiling water over them and let the noodles soften for about 2 minutes. Drain and refresh in cold water. Drain again and set aside.

In a small saucepan, heat together the bean sauce, rind, juice, and rice wine. Heat to a simmer and cook for 2 minutes. The liquid should reduce to ⅓ cup. Remove from the heat and stir in the scallions; cool to room temperature.

Place about ⅓ cup of the noodles in each of the lettuce leaves. Top with a spoonful of the black bean sauce. Scatter the chopped tangerine or orange pieces over the noodles. Serve at room temperature.

Makes 6 servings

Per Serving:
103 Calories; 4g Protein; 1g Fat; 20g Carbohydrates; 0 Cholesterol; 133mg Sodium; 1g Fiber.

Quick Asian Cucumber Pickles

These pickles can be served as part of a salad. After one or two days
in the refrigerator, the spices intensify and the cucumber softens,
turning pickles into a condiment.

About 3 medium cucumbers
   (2 pounds), peeled, seeded,
   and cut into 1½-inch chunks
2 teaspoons salt
1 tablespoon peeled fresh
   gingerroot, cut into
   ⅛ × 2-inch matchsticks
1 tablespoon chili bean sauce
¼ cup rice vinegar
Cilantro sprigs

Place the cucumbers in a colander in the sink and sprinkle with salt; stir to mix. Let drain for 30 minutes. Meanwhile, in a medium bowl, mix together all of the remaining ingredients except cilantro.

Lightly rinse the cucumbers and pat dry. Add them to the bowl with the bean sauce mixture and mix well. Serve immediately or refrigerate for up to 3 days. Scatter the cilantro over the pickles before serving.

Makes about 1 quart of pickles

Per ¹/₄ Cup Serving:
7 Calories; 0g Protein; 0g Fat;
2g Carbohydrates; 0 Cholesterol;
37mg Sodium; 0g Fiber.

Mixed Mushrooms with Rice Wine

Serve these savory morsels with toothpicks as an elegant appetizer.

**½ ounce Chinese dried black
mushrooms, soaked in
hot water to cover for
15 minutes**

**1 teaspoon canola or
vegetable oil**

2 teaspoons minced garlic

**½ to 1 teaspoon red pepper
flakes or to taste**

**½ medium white onion, cut into
slivers (about 1 cup)**

2 tablespoons soy sauce

¾ cup rice wine

**8 ounces fresh button
mushrooms, cleaned
and stemmed**

½ cup chopped scallions

Remove the Chinese mushrooms
from the soaking water and
squeeze out the excess liquid. Cut
off the woody stems and discard.
Strain the soaking liquid and
reserve ¾ cup.

In a large wok or skillet, heat
the oil over medium-high heat.
Stir-fry the garlic and red pepper
flakes until fragrant, about 10
seconds. Add the onions and stir-
fry until the onion begins to
soften, about 1 minute.

Pour in the soy sauce, the
reserved mushroom liquid, and
the wine and heat to a simmer.
Add both the fresh and the
reconstituted mushrooms and heat
to a boil. Simmer for 10 minutes,
then reduce the heat to medium-
high and cook until most of the
juices have evaporated, about
5 minutes. Remove from the heat,
transfer to a serving dish, and
cool to room temperature or
refrigerate. Sprinkle with scallions
before serving.

Makes 6 servings

Helpful Hint

*This dish can be refrigerated for
up to 2 days. Return it to room
temperature before serving.*

Per Serving:
67 Calories; 2g Protein; 1g Fat;
8g Carbohydrates; 0 Cholesterol;
397mg Sodium; 1g Fiber.

Scallion Bread

*Slice this earthy, rustic bread into wedges and
serve with any sambal or chutney.*

1½ cups all-purpose white flour
1 teaspoon salt
**½ cup plus 1 tablespoon hot
    water**
½ cup chopped scallions
1½ teaspoons sesame oil
**1 tablespoon canola or
    vegetable oil**

Place the flour and salt in a food
processor. With the machine
running, pour in the water and
process until the dough almost
forms a ball. Add the scallions and
process until a soft ball forms.
Remove the dough from the food
processor and knead by hand on a
floured surface for 1 minute. Cover
the dough with a kitchen towel
and let it rest for 10 minutes.

Roll the dough out on a floured
surface into an 8½-inch square.
Brush with sesame oil. Starting at
the end nearest you, roll the dough
up into a tight jelly roll. Slice the
roll into three equal parts. Roll
each third between two sheets of
plastic wrap into 6½-inch ovals,
⅛ inch to ¼ inch thick.

To make the bread, heat
1 teaspoon of the oil in a medium
nonstick skillet over medium heat.
Place 1 oval piece of dough in the
skillet, and lower the heat to

medium-low. Cover the pan and
fry the bread until golden brown
on the bottom, about 4 minutes.
Remove the cover, turn the bread
and brown the other side. Remove
the bread, add another teaspoon
of oil to the pan, and continue
with the remaining dough.

Cut each bread into 6 triangles.
(They will look like thick tortilla
chips.)

Makes 4 to 6 servings

Helpful Hint

*This dough can be made by hand,
but it is much simpler in the
processor. Also, the dough can be
made several hours ahead and
refrigerated. The dough may be
rolled on a floured surface rather
than the plastic wrap, but the
plastic wrap makes it super easy—
no cleanup and no sticky dough
to contend with.*

Per Serving:
165 Calories; 3g Protein; 6g Fat;
24g Carbohydrates; 0 Cholesterol;
389mg Sodium; 1g Fiber.

Szechuan Vegetable and Sesame Soup

2 teaspoons minced fresh
    gingerroot
2 teaspoons minced garlic
2 tablespoons Asian sesame
    sauce or tahini
1 tablespoon soy sauce
1 teaspoon hot chili oil
4 cups vegetable broth
1 to 2 small scallions, chopped
    (¼ cup)
1 cup broccoli florets
1 cup trimmed and slivered
    snow peas
1 cup canned whole straw
    mushrooms, drained
3 cups (6 ounces dry) cooked
    thin wheat noodles, Chi-
    nese vermicelli, regular
    linguine, or angel hair
    pasta at room temperature
Soy sauce (optional)

In a small bowl, mix together the ginger, garlic, sesame sauce, soy sauce, chili oil, and 1½ tablespoons of the vegetable broth. Fold in the scallions and set the sauce aside.

Heat the remaining vegetable broth in a medium saucepan. Add the broccoli and cook until it is crisp tender, about 3 minutes. Add the peas and mushrooms and cook until heated through.

Place about ½ cup of the noodles in each of 6 bowls. Top with about 1 tablespoon of the sesame sauce mixture. Top with broth and vegetables and serve immediately. Pass additional soy sauce at the table if desired.

Makes 6 servings

Per Serving:
151 Calories; 8g Protein; 3g Fat;
28g Carbohydrates; 0 Cholesterol;
1,143mg Sodium; 1g Fiber.

Fresh Spring Rolls

One 2-ounce package bean
  thread noodles
1 medium carrot, peeled and
  grated (1 cup)
½ medium daikon radish,
  peeled and grated (1 cup)
1 cup shredded white or
  regular cabbage
2 tablespoons chopped peanuts
1 medium bunch cilantro sprigs
Six 8-inch rice papers

SUGGESTED SAUCES

Don Don Sauce (page 69),
  Sweet and Sour Sambal
  (page 132), hoisin sauce, or
  soy sauce

With scissors, cut the noodles into
3-inch lengths inside a large paper
bag to prevent dried noodles from
flying around the kitchen. Pour
them into a large bowl and cover
with boiling water. Let soak until
they are transparent and glassy,
15 to 20 minutes; drain in a
colander.

While the noodles are soaking,
place the rest of the ingredients,
except the rice papers, in separate
piles on a large platter.

A few minutes before serving,
brush each rice paper on both
sides with water to soften. Let sit
until soft and pliable, then fold
them in half and then in half again
and place on a separate plate.

Top the platter with the
noodles and serve it with the plate
of rice papers and any or all of the
suggested sauces on the side.
Diners unfold a rice paper like a
napkin and place a little sauce and
any of the ingredients inside and
refold it.

Makes 6 servings

Per Serving:
89 Calories; 3g Protein; 2g Fat;
16g Carbohydrates; 0 Cholesterol;
147mg Sodium; 1g Fiber.

Thai Rice Noodle and Ginger Soup

*A traditional Thai first course. Feel free to vary
the noodles according to your taste.*

2 tablespoons soy sauce
2 tablespoons rice vinegar
½ teaspoon brown sugar
6 cups vegetable broth
**1 tablespoon minced fresh
    gingerroot**
1 large shallot, minced
**1 hot green chili, halved and
    seeded**
**1 cup snow peas, trimmed and
    slivered**
**8 ounces rice sticks or
    vermicelli**
2 cups mung bean sprouts
2 tablespoons roasted peanuts
6 large cilantro sprigs
1 lime, cut into 6 wedges

In a small bowl, mix together the soy sauce, vinegar, and sugar. Set aside.

In a medium saucepan, heat the vegetable broth, ginger, shallot, and chili to a simmer. Simmer for 5 minutes, then add the snow peas and cook until wilted, about 30 seconds. Stir in the soy sauce mixture, and simmer for about 10 seconds. Add the rice sticks or vermicelli, and cook until tender, 35 to 40 seconds.

Ladle into serving bowls. Top each bowl with a handful of sprouts, a sprinkling of peanuts, and a cilantro sprig. Serve the lime wedges at the table.

Makes 6 servings

VARIATION

*Substitute almost any noodle for
the rice noodles—lo mein, ramen,
even soba or angel hair. Just cook
until tender.*

Per Serving:
199 Calories; 9g Protein; 3g Fat;
38g Carbohydrates; 0 Cholesterol;
1,473mg Sodium; 2g Fiber.

Thai Lemon Grass and Chili Soup

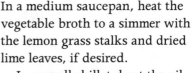

4 cups vegetable broth

2 large lemon grass stalks,
   peeled and cut into 4-inch
   pieces

3 dried Thai keffir lime leaves
   (optional)

1 teaspoon canola or
   vegetable oil

2 teaspoons minced garlic

2 teaspoons roasted chili paste

1½ cups chopped oyster or
   regular mushrooms

2 tablespoons fresh lime juice

2 tablespoons soy sauce

¾ cup finely chopped tomatoes

1 tablespoon minced cilantro

2 to 3 small hot green chilies,
   seeded and halved
   (optional)

In a medium saucepan, heat the vegetable broth to a simmer with the lemon grass stalks and dried lime leaves, if desired.

In a small skillet, heat the oil over medium-high heat. Sauté the garlic until light brown and fragrant, about 30 seconds. When the broth has simmered for 5 minutes, remove the lemon grass and lime leaves and discard. Add the browned garlic to the broth. Heat the soup again to a boil and stir in the chili paste and mushrooms. Cook until the mushrooms have wilted, about 30 seconds, then stir in the lime juice and soy sauce. Remove from the heat and ladle the soup into small bowls.

Top each bowl with a few tomatoes, a little cilantro, and a small pinch of the hot green chilies if desired. Alternatively, the tomatoes and chilies can be mixed together and placed in a small bowl set on the table for people to help themselves.

Makes 6 servings

Per Serving:
35 Calories; 2g Protein; 2g Fat;
4g Carbohydrates; 0 Cholesterol;
1,011mg Sodium; 0g Fiber.

Tofu Dumpling Soup

**7 ounces firm tofu (½ of a
     14-ounce package)**
1 large egg white
½ cup rice flour
2 teaspoons brown miso
1 teaspoon minced ginger
1 teaspoon minced garlic
1 teaspoon sesame oil
4 cups vegetable broth
1 tablespoon soy sauce
2 tablespoons rice wine
**1 cup stemmed and slivered
     fresh shiitake mushrooms**
1 cup spinach leaves

In a medium bowl, mix together the tofu, egg white, rice flour, miso, ginger, garlic, and oil. Mash to a fairly smooth paste. Set aside.

In a medium saucepan, heat the broth, soy sauce, and rice wine to a simmer. Add the mushrooms and cook for 1 minute. Using a table-spoon measure, drop spoonfuls of the tofu mixture into the simmer-ing broth. Poach the dumplings until firm, 2 to 3 minutes. Toss in the spinach leaves and cook until wilted, less than 1 minute. Serve in small bowls.

Makes 12 dumplings, 6 servings

Note

The dumplings will be irregularly shaped. Also, tiny bits of the dumpling may break away. This just adds texture to the broth.

Per Serving:
127 Calories; 7g Protein; 3g Fat;
19g Carbohydrates; 0 Cholesterol;
976mg Sodium; 1g Fiber.

Vegetable Sushi

1 cup short-grained white rice
1¼ cups water
One 3-inch square kombu
1 peeled English, Asian, or
other seedless cucumber, or
2 medium cucumbers,
peeled and seeded
1 bunch spinach, washed and
stemmed, or ½ of a 10-ounce
package prewashed spin-
ach leaves
¼ cup seasoned sushi vinegar
(see Helpful Hints, page 24)
Five 7-inch sheets nori
1 tablespoon wasabi powder
mixed with 1 tablespoon
water
1 tablespoon toasted sesame
seeds (see Helpful Hints,
page 24)
Wasabi
Pickled ginger

For the sushi rice: In a medium saucepan, bring the rice, water, and kombu to a boil. Cover and simmer for 10 minutes. Remove from the heat and continue to let rice steam for 15 minutes without lifting the cover.

Meanwhile, cut the cucumber lengthwise into thin ½-inch strips; set aside.

Place the spinach in a large bowl. Pour boiling water over the spinach and let it sit until wilted, 2 to 3 minutes. Drain and rinse again under cold water. Squeeze the spinach to remove any excess water. (Spinach should be very dry.)

Place steamed rice in a large bowl. Discard the kombu. Fold in the sushi vinegar with a wooden rice paddle or spatula, gently breaking up any clumps. Continue this for several minutes or until the rice cools.

To assemble the sushi, place a sushi rolling mat on a flat surface. Place 1 sheet of nori on the mat. Place about ⅔ cup of sushi rice on the nori, leaving a 1½-inch border. Flatten the rice slightly. Dab about ½ to 1 teaspoon of the thinned wasabi over the rice. Place a few strips of cucumber in the center of the rice. Arrange the spinach in lines on either side of the cucumber slices. Sprinkle with a few sesame seeds.

Starting at one end of the mat, roll it up into a cylinder, removing the mat as you push the roll out. You should have a firm sushi roll. Using a sharp knife, slice it crosswise into 4 or 5 pieces. Serve with a dish of wasabi and pickled ginger.

Makes 5 rolls, 20 to 24 pieces,
about 6 servings

Per Serving:
101 Calories; 3g Protein; 1g Fat;
20g Carbohydrates; 0 Cholesterol;
318mg Sodium; 2g Fiber.

Helpful Hints

Commercially made sushi vinegar is readily available in supermarkets and Asian groceries. If you want to make your own, mix equal amounts of sugar with rice vinegar.

There are so many possible sushi fillings! "Flying" Spinach (page 151) is great in sushi as are any pickled vegetables, bits of mushrooms, or carrot strips.

To toast sesame seeds, place seeds in a small nonstick skillet over medium-high heat. Stir or shake pan until seeds are browned on both sides. Remove from pan immediately to avoid scorching.

Steamed Tofu with Wasabi

**7 ounces firm tofu (half of a
    14-ounce package), drained
    and cut into ½-inch cubes**
1 tablespoon wasabi powder
1 tablespoon water
2 teaspoons shoyu or soy sauce
1 teaspoon sesame oil
1 teaspoon black sesame seeds

Steam the tofu until piping hot,
3 to 4 minutes.

Meanwhile, in a small bowl,
mix together all of the remaining
ingredients except the sesame
seeds. Pour this sauce into a
medium serving bowl or onto a
plate. Place the hot tofu into the
sauce, and sprinkle with the
sesame seeds. Or serve the sauce
on the side.

**Makes about 70 cubes,
approximately 6 servings**

Per Serving:
45 Calories; 4g Protein; 2g Fat;
2g Carbohydrates; 0 Cholesterol;
120mg Sodium; 0g Fiber.

Vegetarian Wonton Soup

6 cups vegetable broth
1 large clove garlic, smashed
1¼ × 2-inch slice peeled ginger-root, smashed
½ recipe Mushroom and Black Bean Wontons (page 9; see Helpful Hint)
½ cup chopped scallions

In a medium saucepan, heat the broth with the garlic and ginger and bring to a boil. Simmer for 10 minutes. Remove the garlic and ginger and discard.

Add the wontons to the broth, and gently simmer for 3 to 4 minutes. Stir in the scallions.

Makes 4 servings

Helpful Hint

The other half of the Mushroom and Black Bean Wontons can be frozen for later. The uncooked, filled wontons will keep up to 2 months in the freezer.

Per Serving:
122 Calories; 7g Protein; 4g Fat; 18g Carbohydrates; 2mg Cholesterol; 1,611mg Sodium; 1g Fiber.

Lumpia

*Lumpia is the Filipino version of fresh egg rolls,
also sometimes called spring rolls. If you prefer to make
your own lumpia wrappers, see the Helpful Hint on page 28.*

**2 tablespoons dark or regular
    soy sauce**
1 teaspoon sesame oil
1 tablespoon black vinegar
**1 medium scallion, chopped
    (about 2 tablespoons)**
**2 teaspoons canola or
    vegetable oil**
1 teaspoon minced garlic
**1 small onion, finely chopped
    (1 cup)**
**1 medium zucchini, chopped
    (1 cup)**
**1 cup chopped bok choy or
    napa cabbage**
**1 cup chopped fresh
    mushrooms**
6 large lettuce leaves
1 cup mung bean sprouts
**6 lumpia wrappers, prepared
    Mandarin pancakes, or
    flour tortillas**

In a small bowl, mix together the
soy sauce, sesame oil, vinegar, and
scallion. In a large wok or skillet,
heat the oil over medium heat.
Stir-fry the garlic for 10 seconds.
Add the onion and stir-fry until it

softens slightly, about 1 minute.
Add the zucchini and bok choy
and stir-fry until the greens are
wilted and the onion is soft, about
2 minutes. Add the mushrooms
and cook until tender, about
2 minutes.

Remove the pan from the heat
and stir in the soy sauce mixture.
(The vegetables should absorb the
liquid almost immediately.) Cool
slightly and transfer to a serving
bowl. To serve, place the lettuce
leaves, bean sprouts, and lumpia
wrappers on a platter.

To make the lumpia, line a
lumpia wrapper with the lettuce
leaf, add about ¼ cup of the
vegetable filling, and top with a
few bean sprouts.

Fold up the lumpia like an
envelope: Place one corner of the
lumpia wrapper over the filling,
fold in the side corners, and roll
up. Diners may fold up their own
lumpia or the lumpia may be
served already prepared.

Makes 6 servings

Per Serving:
333 Calories; 15g Protein; 6g Fat;
58g Carbohydrates; 4mg Cholesterol; 2,396mg Sodium; 7g Fiber.

Helpful Hint

If you prefer to make your own lumpia wrappers, blend 1 egg plus 1 egg white, ⅓ cup cornstarch, and ⅔ cup cold water in a blender; blend until the batter is very smooth. Heat a nonstick 8-inch skillet over medium heat. Pour in ¼ cup batter and tilt the pan to cover the bottom of the skillet completely with the batter.

Cook for about 1½ minutes, then turn the pancake and cook for 10 seconds. Slide the pancake out of the pan and continue making 5 more pancakes in the same way. Keep the lumpia lightly covered with a damp kitchen towel while you prepare the filling. This will make 6 lumpia wrappers.

CHAPTER 2

Main Dishes: Vegetables

Potato and Sea Vegetable Stew

You'll often find one-pot suppers in Japanese kitchens. This particular one is especially good in winter because of its savory flavors.

3 dried shiitake mushrooms, soaked in boiling water for 15 minutes and drained
2¾ cups vegetable broth
½ cup sweet rice wine or mirin
½ medium onion, chopped (about ½ cup)
1 pound each white and sweet potatoes, cut into 1-inch cubes
1 piece wakame, soaked in boiling water for 15 minutes and drained
2 tablespoons dark miso
1 cup spinach leaves, tightly packed
2 teaspoons toasted sesame seeds (see Helpful Hint, page 24)

Trim the woody stems of the shiitake mushrooms and discard. Slice mushrooms into thin slivers.

Meanwhile, in a large saucepan, bring 2½ cups of the broth and the rice wine to a simmer. Stir in the onion and potatoes. Cover and simmer for 5 minutes. Add the mushrooms and wakame.

In a cup or small bowl, mix together the miso and remaining ¼ cup broth and add it to the pot. Simmer the stew, uncovered, until the potatoes are tender, 7 to 10 minutes.

Stir in the spinach and cook until just wilted, about 10 seconds. Ladle the stew into bowls and sprinkle with a few sesame seeds before serving.

Makes 6 servings

Per Serving:
204 Calories; 5g Protein; 2g Fat; 45g Carbohydrates; 0 Cholesterol; 928mg Sodium; 5g Fiber.

Spring Asparagus Foo Yung

1 pound fresh asparagus,
    trimmed and cut diagonally
    into 2-inch pieces
⅓ cup plus 2 tablespoons
    minced scallions
2 teaspoons sesame oil
3 tablespoons soy sauce
2 tablespoons rice vinegar
½ teaspoon hot chili oil
1 teaspoon plum sauce or honey
1 large egg plus two large egg
    whites
1 teaspoon Pepper Salt
    (page 146)
1 teaspoon canola or
    vegetable oil
2 teaspoons minced fresh
    gingerroot
1 teaspoon white sesame seeds
4 cups hot cooked rice

Drop the asparagus into a large pot of lightly salted boiling water for 2 minutes. Drain and immediately place the asparagus in ice water. Drain again and set aside in the colander.

In a small serving bowl, mix together 2 tablespoons of the scallions, 1 teaspoon of sesame oil, the soy sauce, vinegar, chili oil, and plum sauce. Set aside.

In a medium bowl, mix together the egg and egg whites, remaining scallions, Pepper Salt, and the remaining teaspoon of sesame oil.

In a 10-inch nonstick skillet or sauté pan, heat the oil over medium-high heat. Add the ginger and stir-fry for 30 seconds. Add the asparagus and stir-fry for 30 seconds to coat it with the ginger. Then spread the asparagus in 1 layer on the bottom of the pan. Pour in the egg mixture and tilt the pan to coat the bottom. Cover the pan and cook over medium heat until the eggs are just set, about 3 minutes. Uncover the pan and cook until the bottom has browned, 3 to 4 minutes more.

Ease the omelet onto a serving plate. Sprinkle with sesame seeds. Serve with the sauce and the rice on the side.

**Makes 4 servings
(6 as a side dish)**

Per Serving:
319 Calories; 11g Protein; 6g Fat; 55g Carbohydrates; 53mg Cholesterol; 892mg Sodium; 3g Fiber.

Asian Bean Pot

This alternative to Western chili is wonderful warm winter eating.

½ cup vegetable broth
2 tablespoons Chinese rice wine or dry sherry
2 teaspoons canola or vegetable oil
2 teaspoons minced fresh gingerroot
2 teaspoons minced garlic
½ teaspoon red pepper flakes
2 teaspoons fermented black beans
1 medium onion, chopped (about 1½ cups)
2 cups cooked kidney beans, drained
2 cups cooked mung beans, drained
2 tablespoons soy sauce
1 cup fresh or frozen thawed peas
1 teaspoon sesame oil
1 cup minced scallions
Hot cooked rice
Soy sauce (optional)

In a small bowl, mix together the broth and wine.

In a large wok or skillet, heat the oil over medium heat. Stir-fry the ginger, garlic, red pepper flakes, and black beans until fragrant, about 30 seconds. Add the onion and stir-fry until softened, about 1 minute. Add the kidney beans and mung beans and stir-fry for 30 seconds.

Pour in the broth mixture and soy sauce and simmer for 5 minutes. (The beans will absorb most of the broth.) Add the peas and stir-fry for 1 minute. Stir in the sesame oil and scallions and serve immediately over hot cooked rice. Garnish with soy sauce if desired.

Makes 6 servings

Per Serving:
219 Calories; 13g Protein; 3g Fat; 37g Carbohydrates; 0 Cholesterol; 502mg Sodium; 11g Fiber.

Buddha's Delight

A regular on every Chinese restaurant menu.
This version is easy to do at home.

One 2-ounce package bean thread noodles, soaked in hot water for 10 minutes

6 small Chinese dried black mushrooms, soaked in hot water for 10 minutes and drained

1 teaspoon canola or vegetable oil

8 ounces button mushrooms, stemmed

One 12-ounce can baby corn, drained

One 8-ounce can straw mushrooms, drained

2 cups shredded savoy cabbage

3 ounces unflavored seitan, drained and cut into slivers (see Helpful Hint)

½ cup vegetable broth

1 tablespoon soy sauce

4 ounces firm tofu, cut into ½-inch cubes

1½ cups snow peas, soaked in boiling water for 5 minutes and drained

8 ounces oyster or button mushrooms, coarsely chopped

1 teaspoon hot chili oil

1 tablespoon minced cilantro

3 cups hot cooked rice

Drain the noodles in a colander. While they are in the colander, roughly cut them with scissors into 3- to 4-inch lengths. Remove the woody stems from the Chinese mushrooms and discard; slice the mushrooms into slivers.

In a large wok or skillet, heat the oil over medium-high heat. Stir-fry the Chinese and button mushrooms until softened, about 2 minutes.

Stir in the corn, straw mushrooms, cabbage, and seitan. Pour in the broth and soy sauce. Heat to a simmer and cook until the cabbage wilts, about 3 minutes. Then stir in the tofu, bean thread noodles, snow peas, and oyster mushrooms. Stir-fry until the noodles are glassy and transparent. Remove from the heat and stir in the hot chili oil and cilantro. Serve over hot cooked rice.

Makes 6 servings

Helpful Hint

If only flavored seitan is available, drain off flavored liquid before using.

Per Serving:
278 Calories; 15g Protein; 4g Fat; 49g Carbohydrates; 0 Cholesterol; 368mg Sodium; 4g Fiber.

Burmese Chickpea Fritters

Serve these "pancakes" warm with a crunchy cucumber and sprouts salad or simply with a plate of sprouts and any of the spicy sambals.

1 cup sweet rice flour
½ cup chickpea flour
1 cup roughly chopped mung
　　bean sprouts
2 cups cooked white or sweet
　　potatoes, cut into ½-inch
　　cubes
1 teaspoon baking powder
1 teaspoon salt
½ teaspoon turmeric
1½ cups water
1 tablespoon lime juice
2 to 3 teaspoons canola or
　　vegetable oil
Any spicy sambal: Spicy Tomato
　　(page 54), Mint (page 8), or
　　Sweet and Sour (page 132)

In a large bowl, mix together the flours, sprouts, potatoes, baking powder, salt, and turmeric. Stir in the water and lime juice to form a thick batter.

In a large nonstick skillet, heat 1 teaspoon of the oil over medium-high heat. Scoop the batter into the skillet ⅓ cup at a time. Fry until golden brown on both sides, 3 to 5 minutes per side. Continue until you have used all of the batter, adding oil to the pan as necessary.

Makes 6 servings

Per Serving:
146 Calories; 4g Protein; 2g Fat;
28g Carbohydrates; 0 Cholesterol;
460mg Sodium; 2g Fiber.

Vegetable Packets with Southeast Asian Herb Paste

This authentic dish is usually cooked over hot coals. You can also bake this in the oven. The flavor will be decidedly less authentic, but still tasty.

1 recipe Southeast Asian Herb Paste (page 36)
6 large, fresh shiitake mushrooms
2 cups green beans, cut into 3-inch lengths
2 cups snow peas
1 medium red onion, sliced into ¼-inch rings
3 cups greens, such as mizuna or mustard greens, and fresh herbs such as cilantro, basil, or mint
1 bunch scallions (7 or 8), cut into 3-inch pieces
1 banana pepper or yellow bell pepper, cut into 2-inch squares
2 tablespoons coconut milk
1 teaspoon sesame oil
Hot cooked sticky rice or regular rice
Soy sauce
1 large lime cut into thin wedges

Preheat grill, or preheat oven to 450°F. Lightly oil a 14-inch square of foil.

In a large bowl, mix together half of the herb paste and all of the remaining ingredients except for the rice, soy sauce, and lime. Transfer the mixture to the piece of foil and fold the foil over the mixture to form a tight packet.

Place the packet on the grill and cook for 15 to 20 minutes. Alternatively, bake the packet in the oven for 15 to 20 minutes. Remove from the heat and unwrap at the table. Serve with warm sticky rice. Serve the remaining herb paste, the soy sauce, and the lime on the side.

Makes 6 servings

Per Serving:
119 Calories; 5g Protein; 3g Fat; 15g Carbohydrates; 0 Cholesterol; 35mg Sodium; 7g Fiber.

Southeast Asian Herb Paste

1 tablespoon lime juice, plus
   1 to 2 teaspoons more as
   needed
3 large macadamia nuts, or
   6 cashews
1 teaspoon ground Szechuan
   peppercorns
1 large bunch cilantro
1 large clove garlic
Pinch of cayenne pepper

Place all of the ingredients in a food processor or blender and puree. If necessary, add another 1 to 2 teaspoons lime juice to get a smooth blend.

Makes about ⅔ cup

Per Tablespoon:
13 Calories; 0g Protein; 1g Fat;
1g Carbohydrates; 0 Cholesterol;
2mg Sodium; 0g Fiber.

Bok Choy and Bean Stir-Fry

3 tablespoons vegetable broth
1 tablespoon soy sauce
1 tablespoon rice wine
1 teaspoon canola or
  vegetable oil
1 teaspoon minced garlic
2 teaspoons minced fresh
  gingerroot
1 teaspoon fermented black
  beans
About ⅓ large head bok choy,
  chopped (7 cups)
2 cups lima beans, or one
  10-ounce package frozen
  lima beans, thawed
1 teaspoon sesame oil
2 tablespoons coarsely
  chopped unsalted, roasted
  cashews
3 cups hot cooked rice

In a small bowl, mix together the broth, soy sauce, and wine; set aside.

In a large wok or skillet, heat the oil over medium-high heat. Add the garlic, ginger, black beans, bok choy, and lima beans, and stir-fry until the bok choy is softened, about 45 seconds.

Stir in the broth mixture, cover, and cook for 3 minutes over medium-high heat. Remove the cover and stir-fry until the bok choy stems are just tender, 1 to 2 minutes.

Stir in the sesame oil and remove from the heat. Place the vegetables in a serving dish and sprinkle with the cashews. Serve immediately with the rice.

Makes 6 servings

Per Serving:
200 Calories; 7g Protein; 3g Fat;
36g Carbohydrates; 0 Cholesterol;
233mg Sodium; 5g Fiber.

Long- and Short-Bean Stew

Yard-long beans, also called Chinese green beans, are paired here with tiny mung beans (the "short" beans).

2 teaspoons canola or
    vegetable oil
1 tablespoon minced garlic
1 small onion, chopped (1 cup)
2 cups yard-long or regular
    green beans, trimmed and
    cut into 2-inch pieces
One 14-ounce can tomatoes,
    roughly chopped, ½ cup
    juice reserved
Salt and freshly ground
    black pepper
3 cups cooked mung beans
One 10-ounce package fresh
    spinach, or 1 large bunch,
    cleaned and stemmed
1 tablespoon lime juice
3 cups hot rice
1 large lime, cut into thin
    wedges

In a large wok or skillet, heat the oil over medium-high heat. Stir-fry the garlic and onion until the onion softens slightly and the garlic is light golden, about 1 minute. Add the green beans and tomatoes with their juice and reduce the heat to a simmer. Season lightly with salt and pepper.

Cook until the beans are just tender, about 5 minutes. Then add the mung beans and spinach and stir-fry until the spinach is wilted and the mung beans are heated through, about 1 minute. Stir in the lime juice and serve over rice, garnished with lime wedges.

Makes 6 servings

Per Serving:
275 Calories; 12g Protein; 2g Fat;
52g Carbohydrates; 0 Cholesterol;
378mg Sodium; 12g Fiber.

Malaysian Mung Bean and Vegetable Cakes

*These pancakes, usually served with other vegetable dishes and rice,
are popular street-food dinners in the Malaysian markets.*

1 cup whole mung beans,
   soaked in boiling water for
   15 minutes and drained
⅔ to ¾ cup water
½ cup coarsely chopped mung
   bean sprouts
¼ cup chopped scallions
2 tablespoons rice flour
½ cup minced onion
1 tablespoon soy sauce
½ teaspoon baking soda
1 teaspoon sesame oil
1 teaspoon white sesame seeds
2 to 3 teaspoons canola or
   vegetable oil
Distilled white vinegar or soy
   sauce to taste (optional)

Drain the beans and place them in a food processor. Add ⅔ cup of the water and puree. Add up to ¾ cup water if necessary to get a fairly smooth puree. Transfer puree to a large bowl.

Add the bean sprouts, scallions, rice flour, onion, soy sauce, baking soda, sesame oil, and sesame seeds; mix well.

In a large nonstick sauté pan or skillet, heat 1 teaspoon of the oil over medium heat. Add ½ cup of the batter at a time to make ½- to ¼-inch-thick pancakes that are 5½ to 6 inches in diameter. Cook over medium heat until golden brown on each side, about 3 minutes per side. Serve hot with vinegar or soy sauce if desired.

**Makes 6 substantial pancakes,
6 servings**

Per Serving:
78 Calories; 3g Protein; 3g Fat;
11g Carbohydrates; 0 Cholesterol;
175mg Sodium; 3g Fiber.

Thai Potato Curry

2 teaspoons canola or
vegetable oil
1 large onion, chopped (about
1½ cups)
2½ teaspoons Thai Green Curry
Paste, prepared or home-
made (page 41)
1 pound red potatoes, cut into
½-inch cubes
⅓ cup coconut milk
½ cup vegetable broth
1 cup canned whole tomatoes
plus juice
1 tablespoon lime juice
1 tablespoon chopped fresh
basil
3 cups hot cooked rice
Commercially prepared sambal
oelek, optional

In a large wok or skillet, heat the
oil over medium-high heat. Add
the onion and cook until golden,
5 to 7 minutes. Add the curry
paste and stir-fry 1 minute. Add
the potatoes and toss well to coat.
Stir in the coconut milk and
broth.

Using your hands, lightly crush
the tomatoes; add tomatoes and
juice to the wok. Cover and
simmer until the potatoes are
tender, 15 to 20 minutes. Stir in
the lime juice and basil. Serve
over rice with sambal oelek if
desired.

Makes 6 servings

Per Serving:
254 Calories; 5g Protein; 5g Fat;
47g Carbohydrates; 0 Cholesterol;
167mg Sodium; 3g Fiber.

Thai Green Curry Paste

2 teaspoons lemon zest
2 tablespoons chopped cilantro
1 large clove garlic
1 medium shallot, roughly
   chopped
1 small hot green chili pepper,
   seeded and roughly
   chopped
1 teaspoon ground ginger
½ teaspoon freshly ground
   black pepper
½ teaspoon salt
¼ teaspoon ground nutmeg
1 tablespoon vegetable broth
1 teaspoon canola or
   vegetable oil

Place all of the ingredients in a blender or food processor and process to a coarse paste. Store, covered, in the refrigerator for up to 1 week.

Makes about ⅓ cup

Per Teaspoon:
4 Calories; 0g Protein; 0.3g Fat;
0g Carbohydrates; 0 Cholesterol;
83mg Sodium; 0g Fiber.

Quick Potstickers

*Great as a main dish or an appetizer, potstickers are simple to prepare.
(Don't let these seemingly daunting instructions fool you.)*

3 Chinese dried black mushrooms, soaked for 20 minutes in warm water and drained
½ cup finely chopped tempeh or seitan
¼ cup chopped scallions
½ cup mung bean sprouts
½ cup cooked or frozen and thawed spinach, well drained and squeezed dry
½ cup sliced water chestnuts
1½ tablespoons Chinese rice wine or dry sherry
1 tablespoon brown bean sauce, or 2 heaping tablespoons hoisin sauce
1 teaspoon Pepper Salt (page xxx)
1 small package (24 wrappers) round potsticker or Chinese dumpling (siu mai) wrappers
1 tablespoon canola or vegetable oil
⅓ cup water
Prepared plum sauce or Spicy Mustard (page 114)

Remove the woody stems from the mushrooms and discard. Coarsely chop the mushrooms and place in a food processor. Add the tempeh, scallions, sprouts, spinach, and water chestnuts. Pulse to form a chunky paste. Transfer this mixture to a bowl and stir in the wine, bean sauce, and Pepper Salt.

To make the potstickers, moisten a wrapper with water. Place a generous 2 teaspoons of the mushroom mixture in the center, fold the wrapper in half to form a crescent, and seal the edges by pressing them together with your fingers. Continue with the remaining filling until you have used all of the wrappers.

To cook the potstickers, heat 1 teaspoon of the oil in a large nonstick sauté pan or skillet over medium-high heat. Place as many potstickers as will fit without crowding the pan and brown until golden, about 5 minutes. Stir in ⅓ cup water, cover, and reduce the heat to medium. Steam the potstickers for another 5 minutes. (Almost all of the water will evaporate.) Serve immediately with the plum sauce or Spicy Mustard.

**Makes 24 potstickers,
6 servings**

Per Serving:
42 Calories; 2g Protein; 1g Fat; 7g Carbohydrates; 1mg Cholesterol; 59mg Sodium; 0g Fiber.

Sweet and Sour Asian Cabbage Stew

This stew can be found in small bars as well as on formal dinner tables throughout Bali.

2 teaspoons vegetable or canola oil
1 large onion, chopped
1 tablespoon minced fresh gingerroot
1 small hot green chili pepper, seeded and minced
½ large head napa cabbage, cut into 1-inch strips (about 8 cups)
Salt and freshly ground black pepper
1 cup roughly chopped pineapple
1 cup pineapple juice
2 tablespoons rice vinegar
2 tablespoons lime juice
1 tablespoon soy sauce
1 cup cherry tomato halves
1 cup cooked green beans, cut into 1-inch pieces
1 tablespoon chopped cilantro leaves
4 cups hot cooked rice

In a large wok or skillet, heat the oil over medium heat. Add the onion, ginger, and chili and stir-fry until the onion begins to turn golden, about 5 minutes. Add the cabbage and stir-fry to coat. Season with salt and pepper to taste.

After 2 minutes, stir in the pineapple and juice, vinegar, lime juice, and soy sauce. Cover and reduce the heat to medium-low. After 10 minutes, uncover and cook for 10 minutes. Then increase the heat to medium-high and stir in the tomatoes, green beans, and ½ tablespoon of the cilantro. Cook until flavors are well blended and some of the juices have evaporated.

Serve over rice. Garnish with the remaining ½ tablespoon cilantro.

Makes 8 servings

Per Serving:
168 Calories; 4g Protein; 2g Fat; 35g Carbohydrates; 0 Cholesterol; 150mg Sodium; 2g Fiber.

Thai-Style Sweet Potato Stew

The contrast of the hot curry and sweet coconut is a surprising treat with the sweet potatoes.

2 teaspoons canola or
    vegetable oil
1 tablespoon Thai Green Curry
    Paste, prepared or home-
    made (page 41)
1 medium onion, thinly sliced
1 large yam or sweet potato
    (1¼ pounds), peeled, sliced
    in half lengthwise, and then
    cut into ¼-inch half-rounds
    (about 4 cups)
¾ cup vegetable broth
2 tablespoons coconut milk
1 tablespoon soy sauce
1½ cups chopped fresh
    pineapple
1 tablespoon minced cilantro
Hot rice (optional)

In a large wok or skillet, heat the oil over medium-high heat. Stir-fry the curry paste until fragrant, about 10 seconds. Add the onion and stir-fry until it begins to soften, about 3 minutes. Add the yam and stir-fry to coat, about 15 seconds.

Stir in the broth and coconut milk. Bring to a boil and lower the heat to a simmer. Cover and simmer for 10 minutes. Stir in the soy sauce. Increase heat to medium, cover, and cook for 5 minutes.

Stir in the pineapple and cilantro and cook for 30 seconds, stir-frying to mix everything together. Serve over rice if desired.

Makes 4 servings (6 with rice)

Per Serving:
130 Calories; 2g Protein; 4g Fat;
22g Carbohydrates; 0 Cholesterol;
450mg Sodium; 2g Fiber.

Tempura Vegetables

A Japanese favorite. Select 3 or 4 varieties of vegetables from the ingredient list. And don't let the fact that this is deep-fried concern you. You'll use only a fraction of the oil—about two tablespoons—if you remember to heat your saucepan or wok to 360°F before frying.

2 cups all-purpose flour
2 cups ice water
1 teaspoon baking soda
1 cup vegetable broth
2 tablespoons soy sauce
2 tablespoons sake
1 teaspoon brown sugar
2 cups canola or vegetable oil

POSSIBLE VEGETABLES

12 green beans
12 snow peas
12 thin lengthwise slices sweet
   potato
12 baby carrots
6 stalks asparagus
1 medium zucchini, halved
   lengthwise, cut into 6 sticks
6 to 12 small button mushrooms
6 to 12 sweet red, yellow, or
   green bell pepper strips
6 thin wedges of Asian eggplant or thin half-rounds of
   regular eggplant

TO SERVE

Hot cooked rice (optional)

Preheat the oven to 150°F.

Make the coating: In a large bowl, roughly blend together the flour, water, and baking soda. (It should be somewhat lumpy.) Set aside.

Assemble the sauce: In a small saucepan, heat the broth, soy sauce, sake, and sugar to a simmer. Pour into a small serving bowl and set aside.

In a 4-quart saucepan or medium wok, heat the oil over medium heat to 360°F. While the oil heats, assemble the desired vegetables, a cooling rack, and a baking sheet next to the stove. Place the rack on the baking sheet and line the rack with paper towels.

When the oil is hot, place a few vegetables in the batter to coat them. Lift them out of the batter, let the excess batter drip back into the bowl, and lower the coated vegetables into the hot oil. Cook until brown, about 1 minute. Transfer to the towel-lined rack. Keep cooked vegetables warm in the oven while cooking the remaining tempura. Serve with the sauce, and the rice if desired.

Makes 6 servings

Per Serving:
249 Calories; 6g Protein; 5g Fat; 45g Carbohydrates; 0 Cholesterol; 786mg Sodium; 3g Fiber.

Summer Fritters

½ cup distilled white vinegar
2 teaspoons minced garlic
1 cup all-purpose white flour
½ cup cornstarch
½ teaspoon salt
¼ teaspoon freshly ground
    black pepper
1 teaspoon baking powder
1 cup vegetable broth
1 large egg, lightly beaten
1 teaspoon minced fresh
    gingerroot
2 medium summer squash,
    chopped (2 cups)
1 medium bunch scallions, cut
    into 2-inch lengths (about
    ½ cup)
1 cup mung bean sprouts
2 teaspoons canola or
    vegetable oil

Preheat the oven to 175°F.

In a small bowl, mix together the vinegar and garlic. Set aside.

In a large bowl, mix together the flour, cornstarch, salt, pepper, and baking powder. In another small bowl, stir together the broth and egg; stir this into the dry ingredients. Then thoroughly mix in the ginger, squash, scallions, and sprouts.

In a large nonstick griddle or skillet, heat the oil over medium-high heat. Using a ⅓-cup measure, pour the batter onto the griddle or skillet, forming 4-inch fritters. Do not crowd the pan. Cook until golden brown on each side, 2 to 3 minutes per side. Place them in the oven to keep warm while you continue making fritters with the remaining batter. Serve with the garlic-vinegar sauce.

Makes 12 fritters, 6 servings

Per Serving:
162 Calories; 4g Protein; 2g Fat; 30g Carbohydrates; 36mg Cholesterol; 182mg Sodium; 2g Fiber.

Stir-Fry of Spring Onions, Mung, and Fava Beans

This stir-fry is found on formal banquet tables
throughout Thailand. It's best in summer when fava beans are fresh.
(Use canned if you need to, but drain well.)

2 tablespoons coconut milk
¼ cup vegetable broth
1 tablespoon soy sauce
2 teaspoons canola or
vegetable oil
2 teaspoons minced fresh
gingerroot
1 teaspoon minced garlic
1 hot red chili pepper, seeded
and minced
1 cup roughly chopped spring
onions or scallions
2 cups fresh fava beans or
2 cups canned fava beans,
drained
1 cup cooked mung beans
½ cup fresh corn kernels or
½ cup frozen corn kernels,
thawed
4 cups cooked rice
1 cup mung bean sprouts
1 tablespoon lime juice
Mint Sambal (page 18),
commercially prepared
sambal oelek, or
commercially prepared
chili sauce

In a small bowl, mix together the coconut milk, broth, and soy sauce. Set aside.

In a large wok or skillet, heat 1 teaspoon of the oil over medium-high heat. Stir-fry the ginger, garlic, and chili until fragrant, about 30 seconds. Add the onions, fava beans, mung beans, and corn and stir-fry for 30 seconds. Stir in the coconut milk mixture.

Reduce the heat to medium, cover, and simmer until the fava beans are just tender, 3 to 5 minutes. (Almost all of the liquid will have evaporated.)

Add the remaining teaspoon of oil and the rice. Increase the heat to medium-high and stir-fry for 2 to 3 minutes to heat and brown the rice.

Remove the pot from the heat and stir in the sprouts and lime juice. Serve with the sambal or chili sauce on the side.

Makes 6 servings

Per Serving:
283 Calories; 11g Protein; 3g Fat; 53g Carbohydrates; 0 Cholesterol; 353mg Sodium; 7g Fiber.

Stir-Fried Hot Spiced Pineapple and Vegetables

Be sure to select the sweetest pineapple you can find. How do you know whether it's sweet? By smelling it. It should have a fragrant aroma, not a "fermented" one.

2 teaspoons canola or
  vegetable oil
2 medium shallots, very thinly
  sliced
1 teaspoon ground cinnamon
½ teaspoon ground nutmeg
½ teaspoon Chinese five-spice
  powder
2 teaspoons brown sugar
1 hot green chili pepper, seeded
  and minced
1 medium pineapple, cut into
  1-inch cubes (about 5 cups)
¼ cup vegetable broth
¼ cup rice wine
2 cups cauliflowerets
4 cups chopped cabbage
4 cups yard-long or regular
  green beans, cut into 2-inch
  pieces
12 cherry tomatoes, halved
2 tablespoons coconut milk
2 teaspoons minced mint
  leaves
3 to 4 cups cooked rice
Commercially prepared sambal
  oelek or chili sauce

In a large wok or skillet, heat the oil over medium heat. Stir-fry the shallots, cinnamon, nutmeg, and five-spice powder until fragrant, about 30 seconds.

Stir in the sugar, chili, and pineapple and cook for 1 minute. Add the broth and wine and simmer over medium-low heat until the juices have almost evaporated and the pineapple has softened, 5 or 6 minutes.

Stir in the cauliflower, cabbage, and beans. Stir-fry about 2 minutes. Stir in the tomatoes and coconut milk, cover, and simmer until the cauliflower and beans are just tender, about 2 minutes.

Remove from the heat and stir in the mint. Serve over rice or alongside the rice with a small dish of sambal or chili sauce.

Makes 6 servings

Per Serving:
267 Calories; 6g Protein; 4g Fat;
56g Carbohydrates; 0 Cholesterol;
174mg Sodium; 8g Fiber.

CHAPTER 3

Main Dishes: Rice

Basic Fried Rice

Every Asian cuisine has its own version of fried rice, and every cook probably has his or her own unique recipe. Here's a basic recipe for fried rice, followed by variations for experimentation.

1 tablespoon canola or
   vegetable oil
1 tablespoon minced fresh
   gingerroot
2 to 3 cups cooked vegetables
   (broccoli, mushrooms,
   cauliflower, carrots, or
   green beans) chopped into
   1-inch pieces
5 medium scallions, greens
   chopped, white parts cut
   into 1-inch lengths
8 cups cooked rice, cold
1 tablespoon soy sauce, plus
   more to taste
1 large egg, beaten, or ½ cup
   soft tofu, coarsely mashed
Sesame oil to taste

In a large nonstick wok or skillet, heat ½ tablespoon of the oil over medium-high heat until very hot. Add the ginger and stir-fry until fragrant, about 15 minutes. Add the vegetables and the white parts of the scallions; stir-fry until heated through, about 1 minute.

Push the vegetables to one side and add the remaining ½ tablespoon of the oil. Add the rice and stir-fry for 3 minutes. Add 1 tablespoon of the soy sauce and stir-fry 30 seconds more.

Make a well in the center and add the egg or tofu and scramble to mix it in thoroughly. Continue to stir-fry until the rice is dry, 3 to 5 minutes. Remove from heat and stir in the chopped scallion greens. Add additional soy sauce to taste. Sprinkle with sesame oil. Serve immediately.

Makes 6 servings

Per Serving:
326 Calories; 8g Protein; 4g Fat;
64g Carbohydrates; 35mg Cholesterol; 194mg Sodium; 2g Fiber.

VARIATIONS

For Chinese-style fried rice, add 2 or 3 reconstituted Chinese dried black mushrooms, chopped, along with the vegetables.

For a Thai version, stir-fry 1 or 2 chili peppers, chopped, and 1 large clove garlic, chopped, along with the ginger; add 1 or 2 tablespoons fresh mint before serving.

For Vietnamese-style fried rice, mince the tender portion of 1 medium lemon grass stalk along with the ginger and stir in 2 tablespoons minced cilantro with the scallion greens.

For an Indonesian version, add 2 medium shallots, minced, and 1 or 2 hot chili peppers, minced, along with the ginger. Sprinkle a healthy squeeze of lemon or lime juice with the sesame oil.

For all variations above, add 1 tablespoon minced garlic along with the ginger, if desired.

Cantonese Rice with Broccoli and Tofu

*This standard Chinese restaurant dish is a snap to prepare
and a great way to use leftovers.*

FOR THE SAUCE

2 teaspoons dark ("toasted")
   sesame oil
1 tablespoon mushroom or
   regular soy sauce
1 tablespoon soy sauce
2 tablespoons dry sherry
½ cup vegetable broth

FOR THE RICE

1 tablespoon canola or
   vegetable oil
1 tablespoon minced fresh
   gingerroot
1 cup chopped scallions (about
   1 medium bunch)
8 ounces firm tofu, cut into
   1-inch cubes
1 large head broccoli (florets
   and stalks), cooked and
   chopped into 1-inch pieces
6 cups cooked rice, cold

In a small bowl, mix together the sauce ingredients and set aside.

To prepare the rice, heat 2 teaspoons of the oil over medium-high heat in a large wok or skillet. Add the ginger and scallions and stir-fry until fragrant, about 30 seconds. Add the tofu and stir-fry gently until light brown, about 3 minutes. (Be careful not to break up the tofu.) Transfer mixture to a plate and set aside.

Add the remaining teaspoon of the oil to the wok or skillet. Add the broccoli and stir-fry for 1 minute. Add the rice and stir-fry until heated through, about 2 minutes. Stir the sauce and pour it into the pan. Stir-fry for 2 minutes more. Just before removing from the heat, gently stir in tofu mixture.

Makes 6 servings

Per Serving:
329 Calories; 13g Protein; 8g Fat;
52g Carbohydrates; 0 Cholesterol;
288mg Sodium; 4g Fiber.

Cardamom Rice Cakes

This Indonesian street food is often served on banana leaves or bamboo plates. Even on china plates, it's still delicious.

2 cups cooked rice, cold
1 large carrot, shredded (1 cup)
¼ small head red cabbage, cored and shredded (2 cups)
1 medium summer squash, shredded (2 cups)
2 teaspoons minced garlic
2 medium shallots, minced (⅓ cup)
1¼ cups rice flour
1 tablespoon ground cardamom
2 tablespoons soy sauce
½ cup water
½ teaspoon salt
½ teaspoon freshly ground black pepper
2 teaspoons canola or vegetable oil
Spicy Tomato Sambal (page 54)

In a large mixing bowl, combine the rice with the carrot, cabbage, squash, garlic, shallots, and rice flour.

In a separate bowl, mix the cardamom, soy sauce, water, salt, and pepper; add to the shredded vegetable mixture and mix well. Let stand for 5 minutes.

Preheat oven to 175°F.

In a large nonstick skillet, heat 1 teaspoon of the oil. Place ½ cup of the vegetable mixture into the skillet and press it into a round cake about 4 inches in diameter. Cook over medium heat until golden brown on each side, 3 to 4 minutes per side. Keep cooked cakes warm in the oven. Continue cooking until you have used up all of the vegetable mixture. Serve cakes with Spicy Tomato Sambal.

Makes 8 cakes, about 4 servings

Per Serving:
341 Calories; 7g Protein; 4g Fat; 70g Carbohydrates; 0 Cholesterol; 308mg Sodium; 4g Fiber.

Spicy Tomato Sambal

3 small green or red hot chili
   peppers, seeded and
   minced
1 medium tomato, seeded and
   chopped (about ½ cup)
3 tablespoons fresh lime juice
½ teaspoon salt
½ teaspoon cayenne pepper
2 medium shallots, minced
   (about ⅓ cup)
2 teaspoons soy sauce

Place all of the ingredients in a medium bowl and mix well. Let stand 10 minutes before serving. The sambal will keep up to 3 days in a covered container in the refrigerator.

Makes about 1 cup

Per Tablespoon:
4 Calories; 0g Protein; 0g Fat;
1g Carbohydrates; 0 Cholesterol;
159mg Sodium; 0g Fiber.

54

Curry Fried Rice with Leeks, Onions, and Shallots

This pungent, hot, and very aromatic stir-fry is typical of Malaysian cuisine. Serve with a cool salad or simply sliced cucumbers.

FOR THE CURRY PASTE

1 shallot, coarsely chopped
1 hot green chili pepper, seeded
    and coarsely chopped
1 tablespoon coarsely chopped
    fresh gingerroot
¼ cup coconut milk
½ cup vegetable broth
1 tablespoon curry powder
½ teaspoon cinnamon

FOR THE FRIED RICE

4 medium leeks (white part
    only), chopped
½ medium red onion, thinly
    sliced (about 1 cup)
2 medium shallots, thinly sliced
    (about ⅓ cup)
6 cups cooked rice, cold
5 medium scallions, chopped
    (about ½ cup)

In a blender or food processor, process curry paste ingredients into a thin paste.

In a large nonstick wok or skillet, heat the paste to boiling over medium heat. Add the leeks, onion, and shallots and reduce the heat to medium-low. Cook until the onion is soft and the liquid has nearly evaporated, forming a very thick paste, about 5 minutes.

Add the rice and increase the heat to medium. Stir-fry until the rice is golden and heated through. Remove from heat and stir in the scallions. Serve immediately.

Makes 6 servings

Per Serving:
296 Calories; 6g Protein; 4g Fat;
59g Carbohydrates; 0 Cholesterol;
143mg Sodium; 3g Fiber.

Indonesian Eggplant Stew

Javanese eat this stew year-round.

About 4 medium Asian
  eggplants (1 pound)
1 tablespoon kecap manis
  or 1 tablespoon regular
  soy sauce mixed with
  1 teaspoon dark
  brown sugar
2 tablespoons soy sauce
½ cup vegetable broth
¼ cup coconut milk
1 teaspoon canola oil
2 medium shallots, chopped
  (about ⅔ cup)
1 cup thinly sliced onion
1 tablespoon minced fresh
  gingerroot
½ teaspoon red pepper flakes
2 teaspoons minced garlic
2 tablespoons minced cilantro
3 to 4 cups cooked rice, hot

Slice the unpeeled eggplants crosswise into 2-inch pieces. Then cut each piece lengthwise into "fingers." (If the segments are more than 1½ inches thick, cut them in half again lengthwise.)

In a small bowl, mix together the kecap manis, soy sauce, broth, and coconut milk; set aside.

In a large wok or skillet, heat the oil over medium heat. Add the shallots, onion, ginger, red pepper flakes, and garlic and stir-fry until the onion begins to soften, about 1 minute. Add the eggplant and stir until well coated, then pour in the kecap manis mixture and bring to a boil.

Reduce the heat to medium-low, cover, and cook until the eggplant is tender, about 15 minutes. Uncover, increase the heat to medium-high and stir until some of the liquids have evaporated, about 15 minutes. Stir in the cilantro and serve over the rice.

Makes 6 servings

Per Serving:
174 Calories; 5g Protein; 4g Fat;
31g Carbohydrates; 0 Cholesterol;
608mg Sodium; 2g Fiber.

Gado Gado

"Gado gado" literally means "all mixed up," and that's exactly how Indonesia's national dish is served—the ingredients are all mixed up together just before serving.

2 cups shredded napa cabbage
3 cups cooked rice at room
    temperature
1 medium cucumber, peeled,
    seeded, and thinly sliced
    (about 1 cup)
2 cups cooked green beans
2 cups cooked cauliflowerets
1 cup bean sprouts
1 medium carrot, shredded
    (about 1 cup)
6 ounces broiled tempeh sticks,
    optional
2 medium red potatoes, boiled
    and thinly sliced (about
    2 cups)
Spicy Peanut Dressing
    (page 58)

Place the cabbage in a large serving bowl. Arrange the remaining ingredients except the Spicy Peanut Dressing on the cabbage. Toss the salad at the table with the Spicy Peanut Dressing or serve the dressing on the side.

Makes 8 servings

Per Serving:
142 Calories; 4g Protein; 1g Fat; 31g Carbohydrates; 0 Cholesterol; 144mg Sodium; 4g Fiber.

Spicy Peanut Dressing

⅓ cup chunky natural peanut
    butter
⅓ cup coconut milk
¼ cup lime juice
3 tablespoons chopped cilantro
1 tablespoon brown sugar
1 large clove garlic
½ hot green chili pepper,
    seeded and roughly
    chopped
1 dried Thai keffir lime leaf,
    crumbled (optional)

Place all ingredients in a blender
or processor and process until
smooth. Store dressing in the
refrigerator if making ahead, but
bring to room temperature before
serving.

Makes about 1 cup

Per Tablespoon:
47 Calories; 1g Protein; 4g Fat;
3g Carbohydrates; 0 Cholesterol;
34mg Sodium; 0g Fiber.

Mastersauce Rice

This recipe gets its name from the aromatic broth that is used to flavor many Asian dishes.

1 medium leek (white part only), thinly sliced (1½ cups)

1 cup baby carrots, halved lengthwise

6 Chinese dried black mush-rooms (½ ounce), soaked, squeezed dry, and sliced into thin strips

1½ cups rice

3 tablespoons soy sauce

2 teaspoons brown sugar

3 cups vegetable broth

¼ cup dry sherry

½ teaspoon cinnamon

One 2-inch piece of fresh gingerroot, peeled and smashed (see Helpful Hint)

1 piece star anise (1 whole "star")

1 teaspoon sesame oil

In a large saucepan, mix all of the ingredients except the ginger, star anise, and oil. Place the ginger and star anise on top of the mixture. Bring the mixture to a boil over medium heat. Reduce the heat to a simmer and cook until the rice is tender, 20 to 25 minutes. Remove the ginger and star anise. Drizzle with sesame oil and gently fluff the mixture with a fork.

Makes 6 servings

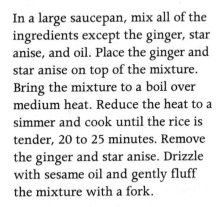

Helpful Hint

To smash ginger, flatten it with the back of a cleaver or wide-blade knife.

Per Serving:
195 Calories; 5g Protein; 2g Fat; 38g Carbohydrates; 0 Cholesterol; 1,081mg Sodium; 1g Fiber.

Balinese Rice Clouds

It's worth making extra Indonesian Festival Rice
and using the leftovers to make the clouds—but in a pinch,
regular rice works just fine.

1 large egg plus 1 large egg
  white
¼ cup chopped scallions
2 teaspoons minced fresh
  gingerroot
1 teaspoon baking powder
½ cup rice milk or 1% milk
2 teaspoons minced fresh
  cilantro
2 teaspoons minced fresh basil
2 cups Indonesian Festival
  Rice, cold (page 64) or
  cooked white rice, cold
1 cup all-purpose white flour
2 to 3 teaspoons canola or
  vegetable oil
Winter Tomato Sambal
  (page 135) or purchased
  chutney
1 cup mung bean sprouts

In a large bowl, lightly beat the egg and egg white. Stir in all of the ingredients except the oil, sambal, and sprouts to form a thick batter.

In a large nonstick skillet, heat 1 teaspoon of the oil over medium heat. Using a ⅓-cup measure, pour the batter into the skillet to form patties. Cook until brown on both sides, about 3 minutes per side. Remove from the pan and continue adding oil as necessary, repeating the process with the remaining batter.

Serve with a dish of sambal or chutney and the sprouts on the side.

Makes 6 patties, 6 servings

Per Serving:
185 Calories; 5g Protein; 3g Fat;
33g Carbohydrates; 35mg Cholesterol; 96mg Sodium; 1g Fiber.

Sizzling Pancakes

*These thin vegetable pancakes are more like crepes
and are served with cilantro, lettuce, and soy sauce.*

FOR THE BATTER

½ cup all-purpose white flour
1 cup rice flour
⅓ cup vegetable broth
¼ teaspoon turmeric
⅓ cup coconut milk
1 tablespoon chopped cilantro
2 cups water

FOR THE FILLING

1 teaspoon canola or vegetable
   oil, plus 1 teaspoon to cook
   pancakes
1 medium bunch scallions,
   chopped (1 cup)
2 cups fresh oyster mushrooms,
   chopped
1 tablespoon minced fresh
   gingerroot
Salt and freshly ground black
   pepper
1 tablespoon chopped cilantro
3 cups mung bean sprouts

FOR THE GARNISH

Cilantro sprigs
1 medium head iceberg lettuce,
   roughly chopped
Soy sauce

Make the batter: Blend all ingredients together in a large mixing bowl and let stand 5 minutes. (The batter will be very thin.)

Make the filling: In a large wok or skillet, heat 1 teaspoon of the oil over medium-high heat. Add the scallions, mushrooms, and ginger and stir-fry until well coated. Season with salt and pepper and stir-fry until the vegetables are browned and wilted, about 3 minutes. Remove from heat, add the cilantro and sprouts, and set aside.

Make the pancakes: Heat an oiled 10-inch nonstick skillet over medium-high heat. When the skillet is hot, pour ½ cup of the filling in the center of the skillet. When it sizzles, pour in ⅔ cup of the batter. Turn the pan quickly to distribute the batter. Cook for about 30 seconds, then reduce the heat to medium and cook until golden, about 2 minutes. (Do not brown the other side.) Gently fold it in half and slide the pancake onto a plate. Continue making pancakes until all batter is used. Serve with cilantro, a platter of crunchy lettuce, and soy sauce.

Makes 6 pancakes, 6 servings

Per Serving:
206 Calories; 6g Protein; 5g Fat;
35g Carbohydrates; 0 Cholesterol;
63mg Sodium; 3g Fiber.

Thai Stir-Fried Rice with Peppers, Mint, and Basil

1 tablespoon canola or
    vegetable oil
2 teaspoons minced garlic
1 tablespoon minced fresh
    gingerroot
2 medium shallots, minced
1 hot green chili, seeded, if
    desired, and minced
Zest of 1 lemon, minced
1 medium sweet red bell
    pepper, chopped into
    1-inch pieces
1 medium sweet yellow or
    green bell pepper, chopped
    into 1-inch pieces
6 cups cooked rice, cold
1 cup chopped scallions
1 tablespoon chopped fresh
    mint
1 tablespoon chopped fresh
    basil
2 tablespoons roasted peanuts,
    chopped (optional)

In a large wok or skillet, heat
2 teaspoons of the oil over
medium heat. Add the garlic,
ginger, shallots, chili, and lemon
zest and stir-fry until fragrant,
about 30 seconds. Add the peppers and stir-fry until crisp
tender, 3 to 5 minutes. Push the
peppers to one side of the pan
and drizzle in the remaining oil.

Add the rice and stir-fry all of
the ingredients until the rice is
heated through. Remove from the
heat and add the scallions, mint,
basil, and peanuts if desired.
Serve immediately.

Makes 6 servings

Per Serving:
240 Calories; 5g Protein; 3g Fat;
48g Carbohydrates; 0 Cholesterol;
42mg Sodium; 2g Fiber.

Indonesian Mixed Fried Rice

NASI GORENG

A delicious and authentic way to use up leftover cooked vegetables and rice.

2 teaspoons canola or
   vegetable oil
3 large shallots, thinly sliced
   (½ cup)
2 teaspoons minced garlic
1 small red hot chili, seeded
   and minced
1 teaspoon tomato paste
2 cups cooked chopped
   broccoli florets
4 ounces grilled, baked, or fried
   tempeh, cut in ½-inch cubes
Salt
4 cups cooked white rice, cold
3 tablespoons kecap manis, or
   3 tablespoons soy sauce
   mixed with 2 teaspoons
   brown sugar
1 cup mung bean sprouts
1 small tomato, cut into thin
   wedges
1 medium cucumber, peeled,
   seeded, and thinly sliced
1 tablespoon shredded coconut
Cilantro sprigs
Winter Tomato, Spicy Tomato,
   or Sweet and Sour Sambal
   (pages 135, 54, and 132)
Additional kecap manis or soy
   sauce

In a large wok or skillet, heat 1 teaspoon of the oil over medium-low heat. Add ¼ cup of the shallots and stir-fry until dark golden brown and crisp, 5 to 7 minutes. (Do not burn.) Remove them from the pan and set aside.

Heat the remaining teaspoon of oil over medium heat and stir-fry the remaining shallots, garlic, chili, and tomato paste for 30 seconds. Add the broccoli and tempeh and stir-fry for 30 seconds. Lightly season with salt. Add the rice and stir-fry 1 minute. Then add the kecap manis and the sprouts. Stir-fry to mix it through and color the rice, about 10 seconds.

Place the tempeh mixture in a large serving bowl and top with the tomato wedges and cucumber slices. Scatter the coconut, reserved shallots, and cilantro sprigs over the top. Serve the rice with small bowls of sambals, and a small pitcher of kecap manis or soy sauce.

Makes 6 servings

Per Serving:
229 Calories; 8g Protein; 3g Fat;
42g Carbohydrates; 0 Cholesterol;
570mg Sodium; 3g Fiber.

Indonesian Festival Rice

NASI KUNING

You'll see this dish at most weddings and funerals and at many Hindu festivals throughout Indonesia. It is often mounded into a large cone shape and surrounded by accompaniments.

1 teaspoon canola or
   vegetable oil
2 teaspoons minced garlic
1 small green chili, seeded and
   minced
½ teaspoon ground cumin
1 teaspoon ground turmeric
2 cups white rice
1 teaspoon salt
⅓ cup coconut milk
5 cups water
3 Thai keffir lime leaves
1 small red bell pepper, cut into
   thin strips
1 small yellow bell pepper, cut
   into thin strips
½ medium cucumber, peeled
   and thinly sliced
1 tablespoon toasted coconut
Spicy Tomato or Sweet and
   Sour Sambal (pages 54
   and 132)

In a large wok or skillet, heat the oil over medium heat. Stir-fry the garlic, chili, and cumin until fragrant, about 20 seconds. Add the turmeric, and after a few seconds add the rice and salt. Stir-fry for about 20 seconds to coat the rice with the spices. Then pour in the coconut milk and water. Top with the lime leaves and bring to a simmer. Cover the pot and cook for 15 minutes. The rice should be barely tender.

Remove the pot from the heat, replace the cover and set aside to let the rice steam for 10 minutes. Remove the lime leaves and discard. Turn the rice mixture out onto a large serving dish and arrange the peppers and cucumbers around the rice. Sprinkle with coconut and serve with sambal.

Makes 6 servings

VARIATION

For a more authentic dish, top with ¼ cup shallots fried to a dark, crispy, golden brown.

Per Serving:
192 Calories; 4g Protein; 5g Fat;
34g Carbohydrates; 0 Cholesterol;
433mg Sodium; 2g Fiber.

Hoisin Rice Pot with Steamed Cabbage Wraps

2 cups rice
2½ cups water
2 cups vegetable broth
1 tablespoon hoisin sauce
2 tablespoons Chinese rice
    wine or dry sherry
6 large white cabbage leaves
1 cup blanched and chopped
    fresh spinach or 1 cup
    thawed and chopped frozen
    spinach
½ cup chopped scallions
½ cup chopped water chestnuts
2 teaspoons minced fresh
    gingerroot
½ teaspoon Pepper Salt
    (page 146)
1 teaspoon sesame oil
Spicy Mustard (page 114) or
    additional hoisin sauce

In a large wok or soup pot, bring the rice, water, broth, hoisin sauce, and wine to a boil. Cover and steam over medium-low heat for 7 to 8 minutes.

Meanwhile, soak the cabbage leaves in boiling water for 15 minutes to soften them. Drain and set aside. In a medium bowl, mix together the spinach, scallions, water chestnuts, ginger, and Pepper Salt. Using a ⅓-cup measure, place a scoop of the spinach mixture in the center of each cabbage leaf and fold up like an envelope.

When the rice has steamed for 7 minutes, or until enough water has evaporated to provide a sturdy surface, place the cabbage rolls on the rice. Continue steaming the rice and cabbage for another 5 to 10 minutes. Remove from the heat and set aside for 5 minutes more.

Transfer the cabbage rolls to a plate and the rice to a large serving bowl. Drizzle the rolls with the sesame oil. Serve the rice and cabbage with Spicy Mustard or a small dish of hoisin sauce for dipping.

Makes 6 servings

Per Serving:
204 Calories; 5g Protein; 2g Fat;
43g Carbohydrates; 0 Cholesterol;
394mg Sodium; 2g Fiber.

Southeast Asian Rice Platter

This dish makes an exquisite party platter, although it's equally appropriate as a quick, light supper. You'll find this dish in the fanciest hotels in Bangkok as well as in the humble homes of Bali.

4 cups cooked rice, room
   temperature or cold
2 tablespoons lemon juice
2 tablespoons light soy sauce
2 teaspoons minced fresh
   gingerroot
2 teaspoons canola or
   vegetable oil
2 teaspoons minced mint
½ hot red chili pepper, seeded
   and minced
½ teaspoon brown sugar
3 tablespoons toasted
   unsweetened coconut
   chips or shreds
1 cup fresh peas or 1 cup
   thawed frozen peas
1 cup cooked green beans, cut
   into ½-inch pieces
½ medium red pepper, seeded
   and diced (1 cup)
1 small Asian apple pear or tart
   apple, cored and coarsely
   chopped (about 1 cup)
1 firm mango, chopped
   (optional)
½ medium head iceberg
   lettuce, shredded
Mint sprigs
1 lime cut into small wedges
Soy sauce

Place the rice in a large bowl. In a separate small bowl, mix together the lemon juice, soy sauce, ginger, oil, mint, chili, and sugar. Pour mixture over the rice. Then stir in 2 tablespoons of the coconut, the peas, beans, pepper, apple pear, and mango if desired.

Place the shredded lettuce on a large serving platter. Pile the rice mixture in the center, leaving a border of lettuce shreds. Scatter the mint sprigs and remaining coconut over the rice. Serve with lime wedges and additional soy sauce.

Makes 6 servings

Per Serving:
217 Calories; 6g Protein; 3g Fat;
42g Carbohydrates; 0 Cholesterol;
223mg Sodium; 4g Fiber.

CHAPTER 4

Main Dishes: Noodles

Tempeh Cubes

This pasta dish is served year-round in Indonesia and Malaysia.

8 ounces regular or multigrain tempeh, cut into ½-inch cubes
½ cup pineapple juice
¼ cup lime juice
1 tablespoon kecap manis or dark soy sauce
1 teaspoon canola oil
¼ teaspoon cayenne pepper
¼ teaspoon ground ginger
Zest of 1 small lime (about 1½ teaspoons)
One 12-ounce package mai fun noodles
2 cups mung bean sprouts
1 large cucumber, peeled, seeded, and cut into 2-inch pieces (about 2 cups)
Cilantro and mint sprigs
Commercially prepared sambal oelek or Spicy Tomato Sambal (page 54)
Additional kecap manis or dark soy sauce

In a medium bowl, mix the tempeh cubes with the pineapple juice, lime juice, kecap manis, oil, cayenne, ginger, and lime zest. Let stand for 10 minutes.

Meanwhile, preheat the oven to 450°F. Place the noodles in a large bowl and cover with boiling water; set aside until noodles are softened, about 2 minutes. Drain immediately in a colander and run cold water over the noodles to cool them. Drain well.

Place the tempeh and ½ cup of the marinade in a lightly oiled baking dish and bake for 5 minutes. Toss the cubes to turn them, and bake another 10 minutes. Alternatively, thread the tempeh cubes onto 8 bamboo skewers and baste with the marinade. Place on a hot grill and cook until crisp and golden, 10 to 12 minutes.

Place the drained and cooled noodles in the center of a large serving plate. Surround the noodles with tempeh cubes or kabobs. Scatter the sprouts and cucumber over the top. Garnish with the cilantro and mint. Serve with dishes of the sambals, kecap manis, or soy sauce.

Per Serving:
233 Calories; 12g Protein; 3g Fat; 41g Carbohydrates; 0 Cholesterol; 234mg Sodium; 3g Fiber.

Makes 8 servings

Asparagus and Don Don Noodle Platter

FOR THE NOODLES

14 ounces firm tofu, cut into 1-inch cubes

1 teaspoon dried lemon grass

2 tablespoons rice vinegar

2 tablespoons soy sauce

6 ounces wide rice noodles, boiled and drained, at room temperature

12 ounces thin asparagus stalks, cooked crisp-tender

½ cup sliced water chestnuts

Additional soy sauce to taste

FOR THE SAUCE

1 teaspoon minced garlic

2 tablespoons natural chunky peanut butter

1 tablespoon soy sauce

1 teaspoon brown sugar

1 teaspoon hot chili oil

2 tablespoons rice wine

2 tablespoons lemon juice

1 tablespoon minced cilantro leaves

Preheat the oven to 400°F. Place the tofu in a nonstick or lightly oiled 9×13-inch baking dish along with the dried lemon grass, rice vinegar, and soy sauce. Gently mix to coat the tofu. Set aside for 15 minutes (or refrigerate for up to 6 hours).

Roast the tofu until heated through, 15 to 18 minutes. While the tofu bakes, prepare the Don Don Sauce. In a small bowl, mix together all of the ingredients for the sauce. (This can be stored for up to 2 days in the refrigerator.)

Place the noodles in the center of a large serving platter. At one end, place the asparagus spears. Place the baked tofu on the platter with the noodles. Scatter the water chestnuts over the top and serve the Don Don Sauce and a little pitcher of soy sauce on the side.

Makes 6 servings

Per Serving (noodles):
173 Calories; 11g Protein; 3g Fat; 26g Carbohydrates; 0 Cholesterol; 480mg Sodium; 2g Fiber.

Per Tablespoon (sauce):
38 Calories; 1g Protein; 3g Fat; 2g Carbohydrates; 0 Cholesterol; 149mg Sodium; 0g Fiber.

Noodle Cake

Ever wonder what to do with leftover cooked noodles or spaghetti?
This noodle cake is fast, easy, and a great base for a stir-fry.
Serve with Black Bean, Broccoli, and Onion Topping (page 71)
or Snow Pea, Leek, and Mushroom Topping (page 72).

**1 tablespoon canola or
vegetable oil**
**3 cups cooked Chinese
vermicelli or very thin
wheat noodles**

In a 10-inch nonstick skillet, heat the oil over medium-high heat. Press the noodles into the pan to form a pancake. Fry until golden brown, about 4 minutes.

Remove from the heat and place a plate over the pan. Flip the noodles onto the plate, then slide the noodles back into the pan, uncooked side down. Brown the underside of the noodles, about 3 minutes. Transfer the cake to a cutting board. Cut into wedges and serve immediately as a base for a stir-fry or with the toppings on the following pages.

Makes 6 servings

Per Serving:
127 Calories; 2g Protein; 2g Fat;
21g Carbohydrates; 0 Cholesterol;
0mg Sodium; 1g Fiber.

Black Bean, Broccoli, and Onion Topping

Serve this on top of or alongside Noodle Cake (page 70).

1 pound broccoli, stems peeled, cut into 4 cups florets and 1 cup stems in 1½-inch pieces
2 teaspoons canola or vegetable oil
1 tablespoon minced fresh gingerroot
1 large onion, cut into quarters, then cut into ⅛-inch slices
½ cup vegetable broth
1 tablespoon black bean sauce
1 teaspoon sesame oil
½ cup chopped scallions
2 tablespoons cilantro leaves

In a large pot of salted boiling water, blanch the broccoli until it turns bright green, about 3 minutes. Drain and rinse under cold water. Drain again and set aside.

In a large wok or skillet, heat the oil over medium heat. Stir-fry the ginger until fragrant, about 20 seconds. Add the onion and stir-fry until it begins to soften and brown, about 3 minutes.

Add the broccoli and stir-fry 1 minute. Stir in the broth and the bean sauce. Cover and simmer over medium-low heat until the broccoli is crisp-tender, 3 to 4 minutes. Sprinkle with the sesame oil, scallions, and cilantro. Serve immediately on top of or alongside the noodle cake.

Makes 6 servings

Per Serving:
55 Calories; 3g Protein; 3g Fat; 7g Carbohydrates; 0 Cholesterol; 105mg Sodium; 3g Fiber.

Snow Pea, Leek, and Mushroom Topping

Use this noodle topping year-round, varying the mushrooms as they are available. Serve over a Noodle Cake (page 70).

4 ounces snow peas (1½ cups)
1 tablespoon fermented bean
   sauce
1 tablespoon soy sauce
¼ cup dry sherry
¼ cup vegetable broth
2 teaspoons canola or
   vegetable oil
1 large shallot, chopped (⅓ cup)
2 teaspoons minced garlic
1 large leek, white part only,
   cut into 1-inch pieces
8 ounces fresh button mush-
   rooms, quartered (3 cups)
1 teaspoon Pepper Salt
   (page 146)

Place the snow peas in a large mixing bowl. Pour in boiling water to cover and set aside for 1 minute to soften. Drain, rinse in cold water, and drain again. Set aside.

In a separate small bowl, mix together the bean sauce, soy sauce, sherry, and broth. In a large wok or skillet, heat the oil over medium-high heat. Add the shallot and garlic and stir-fry until the shallot is light golden, about 30 seconds. Add the leek and stir-fry until it is slightly soft, about 30 seconds. Add the mushrooms and stir-fry 1 minute.

Stir in the bean sauce mixture and cook until the mushrooms are done, about 1 minute. Add the snow peas and stir-fry until heated through, about 15 seconds. Push the vegetables to one side of the pan and allow the juices to reduce and thicken slightly.

Season with Pepper Salt.

Makes 6 servings

Per Serving:
79 Calories; 2g Protein; 2g Fat;
7g Carbohydrates; 0 Cholesterol;
464mg Sodium; 2g Fiber.

Javanese Tomato Noodles

This is as close as you'll come to spaghetti and tomato sauce in Asia.
The rice noodles make it a light dish.

1½ cups tomato sauce
⅓ cup coconut milk
½ teaspoon cayenne pepper
1½ teaspoons mushroom soy
    sauce or regular soy sauce
2 teaspoons chopped cilantro
1 pound wide rice noodles or
    fettuccine, cooked
Cilantro sprigs

In a medium saucepan, heat the tomato sauce, coconut milk, cayenne, and soy sauce to a simmer. Simmer for 5 minutes. Stir in the cilantro and pour the sauce over the hot noodles. Top with a few cilantro sprigs.

Makes 6 servings

Per Serving:
315 Calories; 10g Protein; 3g Fat;
63g Carbohydrates; 0 Cholesterol;
464mg Sodium; 1g Fiber.

Pad Thai

The classic Thai dish.

12 ounces wide, flat rice noodles, soaked in water for 15 minutes
2 tablespoons rice wine
½ teaspoon brown sugar
2 tablespoons soy sauce
1 teaspoon tomato paste
2 teaspoons canola or vegetable oil
2 teaspoons minced garlic
1 small red chili pepper (seeding is optional; see Helpful Hint), minced
1 medium shallot, sliced (¼ cup)
2 cups finely chopped broccoli florets
7 ounces firm tofu, cut into ½-inch cubes
1 large egg, lightly beaten (optional)
2 cups mung bean sprouts
½ cup scallions, cut into 2-inch lengths
1 tablespoon finely chopped roasted peanuts
Prepared Thai chili sauce
1 lime sliced in 6 wedges

In a large pot of boiling water, cook rice noodles until just tender, 30 seconds to 1 minute. Drain and set aside in a colander.

In a small bowl, mix together the rice wine, sugar, soy sauce, and tomato paste; set aside.

In a large wok or skillet, heat the oil over medium-high heat. Add the garlic, chili, and shallot and cook for 10 seconds. Then add the broccoli and stir-fry until it is softened slightly, about 1 minute. Add the tofu and stir-fry 30 seconds.

If using the egg, push the vegetables to the side to make a well in the center of the pan. Pour the egg into the well and cook until just set, then stir-fry the vegetables into the egg.

Add the rice wine mixture, the noodles, half of the sprouts, and the scallions. Cook until just heated through, about 1 minute. Turn out onto a platter and scatter the remaining sprouts and peanuts over the top. Serve with the Thai chili sauce to taste and lime wedges.

Makes 6 servings

Helpful Hint

The seeds of peppers carry a lot of the "heat." Depending on your ability to withstand the blister, you can decide to remove the seeds or not.

Per Serving:
285 Calories; 12g Protein; 4g Fat; 50g Carbohydrates; 0 Cholesterol; 412mg Sodium; 2g Fiber.

Vietnamese Noodle Bowl

PHO

Pho, pronounced far, *is the classic Vietnamese one-meal-in-a-bowl. Pho houses are commonplace in Vietnam and are becoming more popular in metropolitan areas of the United States.*

12 ounces flat rice noodles, soaked in water for 20 minutes and drained
1 large stalk lemon grass, peeled
3 cloves garlic, peeled
One 2-inch piece fresh gingerroot, peeled
1 hot red chili pepper, quartered and seeded
6 cups vegetable broth
1 medium carrot, peeled and sliced into ¼-inch rounds
4 mint sprigs
4 cilantro sprigs
7 ounces firm tofu, cut crosswise into 6 slices
1 tablespoon lime juice, or to taste
Prepared Vietnamese or Thai chili sauce
1 lime, cut into 6 wedges
Soy sauce

Drop the noodles in a large pot of boiling water for 30 seconds. Drain and set aside in a colander.

With a cleaver or the back of a large knife, flatten the lemon grass, garlic, and ginger. Place in a soup pot with the chili, broth, carrot, 2 sprigs of mint, and 2 sprigs of cilantro. Bring to a simmer, cover, and cook for 10 minutes.

Meanwhile, divide the noodles and tofu evenly among 6 deep soup bowls. Add the lime juice to the simmering broth and remove from the heat. Remove the lemon grass, garlic, and chili. Ladle the broth into the bowls. Top with the remaining mint and cilantro and serve immediately with the chili sauce, lime, and soy sauce on the side.

Makes 6 servings

Per Serving:
259 Calories; 12g Protein; 2g Fat; 50g Carbohydrates; 0 Cholesterol; 1,050mg Sodium; 1g Fiber.

Minty Mai Fun

This is particularly good in summer when ripe tomatoes and fresh mint are abundantly available in most local markets.

2 tablespoons distilled white
   vinegar
2 tablespoons soy sauce
2 tablespoons vegetable broth
½ teaspoon brown sugar
2 teaspoons canola or
   vegetable oil
½ teaspoon red pepper flakes
About 2 large leeks, chopped
   (1½ cups)
1 or 2 hot green chili peppers,
   seeded and chopped
   (1 cup)
7 ounces firm tofu, cut into
   ½-inch cubes
One 6-ounce package mai fun
   noodles (thin rice sticks),
   soaked in water for 20
   minutes
1 cup chopped fresh tomatoes
2 tablespoons minced fresh
   mint
1 teaspoon sesame oil
Soy sauce to taste (optional)

In a small bowl, mix together the vinegar, soy sauce, broth, and sugar. Set aside.

In a large wok or skillet, heat the oil over medium heat. Stir-fry the red pepper flakes, leeks, and chili until the vegetables begin to soften, about 2 minutes. Add the tofu and stir-fry for 1 minute. (Don't worry if the tofu crumbles a bit.)

Drain the noodles and add them and the soy sauce mixture to the wok. Stir-fry until the noodles are tender, about 3 minutes. Increase the heat to medium-high, add the tomatoes and 1 tablespoon of the mint, and cook for 30 seconds more. Drizzle on the sesame oil and remove from the heat. Turn out onto a platter and sprinkle with the remaining mint. Serve with a small pitcher of soy sauce if desired.

Makes 6 servings

Per Serving:
165 Calories; 3g Protein; 3g Fat;
31g Carbohydrates; 0 Cholesterol;
461mg Sodium; 1g Fiber.

Cold Sesame Noodle Platter

Feel free to add to the vegetable list.

3 ounces firm or soft tofu
2 tablespoons Asian sesame
    sauce or tahini
2 tablespoons dark soy sauce
2 tablespoons distilled white or
    rice vinegar
1 tablespoon lemon juice
½ teaspoon brown sugar
1 teaspoon hot chili oil
1 tablespoon cilantro, minced
½ teaspoon white sesame seeds
12 ounces cooked lo mein or
    other thin wheat noodles,
    drained and rinsed
1 cup steamed small
    cauliflowerets
1 cup sliced carrots, steamed
1 cup peeled and seeded
    cucumber, cut into 2-inch
    wedges
1 cup mung bean sprouts
Quick Asian Cucumber Pickles
    (page 15), optional

In a large bowl, mix together the tofu, sesame sauce, soy sauce, vinegar, lemon juice, sugar, oil, and cilantro. Place in a serving bowl and top the sauce with the sesame seeds.

Arrange the noodles in the center of a large serving platter or divide among 6 bowls. Surround the platter or top the bowls with the vegetables and bean sprouts. Serve the tofu sauce and Quick Asian Cucumber Pickles, if desired, on the side.

Makes 6 servings

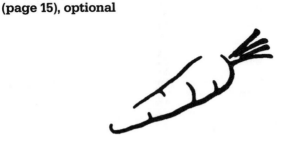

Per Serving:
255 Calories; 9g Protein; 3g Fat;
48g Carbohydrates; 0 Cholesterol;
1,415mg Sodium; 4g Fiber.

Fun See Vegetables

Glassy noodles are elegant and actually great fun to serve. It's magic to watch them turn transparent as they cook.

2 ounces bean thread noodles, soaked for 5 minutes in warm water

6 Chinese dried black mushrooms (½ ounce), soaked for 20 minutes in warm water and drained

2 tablespoons dark soy sauce

⅓ cup vegetable broth

1 teaspoon sesame oil

1 teaspoon canola or vegetable oil

2 teaspoons minced fresh gingerroot

2 cups chopped bok choy (leaves and stems)

1½ cups cauliflowerets

1 medium green bell pepper, seeded and cut into 1½-inch squares

½ cup chopped scallions, cut diagonally into 1-inch pieces

½ cup lotus root, drained and cut into thin rings

One 8-ounce can straw mushrooms, drained

1 cup trimmed snow peas

1 teaspoon Pepper Salt (page 146)

Drain the noodles, and cut into 3-inch lengths. Set aside.

Remove the woody stems from mushrooms and discard. Thinly slice caps.

In a small bowl, mix together the soy sauce, broth, and sesame oil. In a large wok or skillet, heat the canola oil over medium-high heat. Stir-fry the ginger for 10 seconds. Then add the bok choy and stir-fry until it has begun to soften, about 1 minute. Add the cauliflower, pepper, and Chinese mushrooms. Stir-fry until the bok choy begins to brown, about 1 minute. Add the scallions and lotus root and stir-fry for 30 seconds.

Add the straw mushrooms, snow peas, and the soy sauce mixture and bring to a simmer. Add the noodles and stir-fry until the noodles become glassy, about 1 minute. Season with Pepper Salt. Serve immediately.

Makes 6 servings

VARIATION

For a more substantial dish, add 6 ounces of firm tofu, cubed, with the scallions and lotus root.

Per Serving:
104 Calories; 4g Protein; 2g Fat; 19g Carbohydrates; 0 Cholesterol; 535mg Sodium; 4g Fiber.

Vegetable Mee Krob

2 cups canola or vegetable oil
4 ounces dried thin rice
    vermicelli noodles
1 tablespoon soy sauce
2 tablespoons rice vinegar
1 teaspoon tomato paste
¼ to ½ teaspoon cayenne
    pepper
½ cup minced onion
2 teaspoons minced garlic
1 hot green chili pepper, seeded
    and minced
1 large egg plus 2 large egg
    whites, lightly beaten
5 ounces firm tofu (1¼ cups)
½ cup chopped scallions
1 cup mung bean sprouts
Cilantro sprigs

In a large deep wok or soup pot, heat the oil to 360°F.

While the oil is heating, place the dried noodles in a large paper bag. Break up the noodles into small pieces. Assemble a baking sheet lined with paper towels and a skimmer or tongs nearby.

When the oil is hot, put a small handful of the dried noodles into the oil. They will immediately puff up and stick together. Turn over the mass of noodles with the tongs or skimmer so the other side can puff up. Remove the noodles and drain on the paper towels. Continue until you've cooked all of the noodles.

Cool the pan slightly and pour off all but 1 teaspoon of the oil or enough to film the bottom of the pan. Place the pan back on medium heat. While the pan is reheating, mix together the soy sauce, vinegar, tomato paste, and cayenne in a small bowl; set aside.

Add the onion, garlic, and chili to the pan and stir-fry until the onion has softened slightly and the garlic is a light brown, about 1 minute. Add the eggs, tofu, and scallions and cook until the eggs are lightly scrambled, about 20 seconds. Add the soy sauce mixture and cook until the mixture is completely dry, about 1 minute.

Stir in the sprouts and ½ cup of the noodles. (The noodles will soften and break up.) Remove the pot from the heat.

Place the remaining noodles on a large serving platter and make a well in the center. Place some of the cooked mixture in the center and the rest on the crispy noodles, leaving a large border around the edges. Decorate the top with cilantro sprigs.

Makes 6 servings

Per Serving:
156 Calories; 7g Protein; 6g Fat; 19g Carbohydrates; 35mg Cholesterol; 251mg Sodium; 1g Fiber.

Hot and Sour Bean Sauce Noodles

**1 tablespoon fermented bean
 curd**
2 tablespoons mild bean sauce
2 tablespoons soy sauce
2 tablespoons lemon juice
¼ cup vegetable broth
**2 teaspoons canola or
 vegetable oil**
**2 teaspoons minced fresh
 gingerroot**
2 large leeks, chopped (2 cups)
**1 medium head bok choy,
 chopped crosswise into
 ½-inch shreds (8 cups)**
4 cups cooked fettuccine
1 teaspoon hot chili oil
**3 tablespoons minced Chinese
 chives, garlic chives, or
 regular chives**

In a small bowl, mix together the fermented bean curd, bean sauce, soy sauce, lemon juice, and broth.

In a large wok or skillet, heat the oil over medium-high heat. Stir-fry the ginger and leeks until the leeks soften slightly, about 1 minute. Add the bok choy and stir-fry until well coated, about 1 minute. Stir in the bean sauce mixture, reduce heat to medium-low, cover, and simmer 3 to 5 minutes.

Add the fettuccine and chili oil. Toss thoroughly until the fettuccine is heated through. Remove the pan from the heat and stir in 2 tablespoons of the chives. Serve sprinkled with the remaining chives and sauce.

Makes 6 servings

Per Serving:
208 Calories; 7g Protein; 3g Fat;
39g Carbohydrates; 0 Cholesterol;
551mg Sodium; 4g Fiber.

Korean Bean Thread Noodle Stir-Fry

CHAPCHAYE

One 2-ounce package bean thread noodles, cut into 3-inch lengths
2 teaspoons canola or vegetable oil
1 teaspoon minced garlic
½ teaspoon chili powder
2 cups quartered fresh mushrooms
1 cup shredded cabbage
1 cup sliced carrots, cut into 2-inch slivers
½ cup scallions, cut in half lengthwise and then into 3-inch lengths
½ cup vegetable broth
1 tablespoon dark soy sauce
1 cup mung bean sprouts
1 teaspoon sesame oil
2 teaspoons white sesame seeds

Place the noodles in a large bowl and pour boiling water over the noodles to cover. Let the noodles soak while you prepare the rest of the ingredients. (They will become soft and lightly transparent.)

In a large wok or skillet, heat the oil over medium-high heat. Stir-fry the garlic and chili powder until fragrant, about 10 seconds. Add the mushrooms, cabbage, carrots, and scallions and stir-fry for 2 minutes.

Drain the noodles, add them to the pan, and stir-fry for 30 seconds. Then pour in the broth and soy sauce and stir-fry until the noodles are glassy and most of the broth has been absorbed, about 30 seconds. Remove from the heat and stir in the bean sprouts and sesame oil. Transfer to a serving platter and sprinkle with the sesame seeds.

Makes 4 servings

Per Serving:
79 Calories; 3g Protein; 5g Fat;
8g Carbohydrates; 0 Cholesterol;
400mg Sodium; 2g Fiber.

Green Curry and Thai Eggplant Noodles

This curried eggplant dish takes a little longer, but it is very easy!

1 large eggplant, or 8 small Asian eggplants, halved lengthwise
1 tablespoon canola or vegetable oil
1 tablespoon lemon juice
1 teaspoon Thai Green Curry Paste, prepared or homemade (page 41)
½ cup chopped scallions
1½ teaspoons minced garlic
2 tablespoons minced fresh basil
12 ounces medium-width rice noodles, cooked
1 cup halved cherry tomatoes
1 lime, cut into 6 small wedges
Additional soy sauce

Preheat the oven to 375°F. Rub the eggplant with 1 teaspoon of the oil and place on a nonstick or lightly oiled baking sheet, cut side down. Bake until very soft, about 40 minutes for the large eggplant or 25 to 30 minutes for the Asian eggplants.

While the eggplant bakes, mix together the lemon juice, curry paste, scallions, garlic, and 1 tablespoon of the basil. When the eggplant has cooled enough to handle, scoop out the flesh and chop finely. Mix it into the curry mixture and blend well.

If the noodles are not freshly cooked, place them in a bowl and pour boiling water over them to reheat.

In a large wok or skillet, heat the remaining oil over medium-high heat. Fry the eggplant paste for a few minutes until it sizzles and is well blended with the oil. Stir in the tomatoes and cook for another 30 seconds. Remove the pan from the heat. Drain the noodles and divide them among 6 bowls. Spoon the eggplant mixture over the noodles and top each with a little of the remaining basil. Serve with a small plate of lime wedges and a pitcher of soy sauce.

Makes 6 servings

Per Serving:
251 Calories; 2g Protein; 3g Fat;
56g Carbohydrates; 0 Cholesterol;
16mg Sodium; 3g Fiber.

Bean Sauce Noodles with Heaps

*In this case, "heaps" are small piles of vegetables
served with flavored noodles.*

¼ cup chopped scallions
2 tablespoons dark soy sauce
2 tablespoons balsamic vinegar
1 teaspoon sesame oil
½ teaspoon brown sugar
8 ounces fresh wheat linguine
   or fettuccine
2 tablespoons rice wine
3 tablespoons brown bean
   sauce
¼ cup vegetable broth
1 cup mung bean sprouts
½ cup sliced radishes
1 cup steamed snow peas
1 cup chopped tomatoes

In a small serving dish, mix together the scallions, soy sauce, vinegar, sesame oil, and sugar. Set aside.

In a large wok or soup pot, cook the linguine according to package directions until tender; drain. Using the pasta boiling pot, heat the rice wine, bean sauce, and broth to a simmer. Simmer for 1 minute. Turn off the heat and add the drained noodles. Stir to mix everything well and turn onto a large serving platter. Top with little mounds or "heaps" of the vegetables. Serve with the soy dipping sauce on the side.

Makes 6 servings

Per Serving:
164 Calories; 7g Protein; 1g Fat;
32g Carbohydrates; 0 Cholesterol;
490mg Sodium; 6g Fiber.

Hoisin Noodles

2½ tablespoons hoisin sauce

3 tablespoons Chinese rice wine or dry sherry

½ cup vegetable broth

1¾ cups trimmed snow or sugar snap peas (about 6 ounces)

1 pound fresh lo mein or very thin fresh wheat spaghetti

1 teaspoon canola or vegetable oil

2 teaspoons minced fresh gingerroot

⅔ cup sliced water chestnuts

½ cup chopped scallions

1 teaspoon sesame oil

1 tablespoon finely chopped roasted peanuts

Additional hoisin sauce

In a small bowl, mix together the hoisin, wine, and broth; set aside. In a large wok or soup pot, bring 4 quarts of water to a boil. Assemble a bowl of cold water and a skimmer or strainer nearby.

Drop the peas into the boiling water until softened, about 30 seconds, then remove them with the skimmer or strainer and plunge them into the cold water.

Add the noodles to the boiling water. Cook according to package directions until just tender; drain, rinse well with cold water, and set aside to drain.

Wipe the wok dry and place over medium-high heat. Add the oil and ginger and stir-fry for 10 seconds. Reduce the heat to medium and stir in the hoisin mixture. Heat for 30 seconds, then stir in the noodles and toss thoroughly. Add the peas, chestnuts, scallions, and sesame oil and toss again until everything is well mixed and the noodles are hot. Place the mixture in individual bowls or one big serving dish and scatter the peanuts on top. Serve with a small dish of hoisin on the side.

Makes 6 servings

Per Serving:
281 Calories; 11g Protein; 3g Fat; 56g Carbohydrates; 0 Cholesterol; 95mg Sodium; 10g Fiber.

Kim Chee Noodles

*The silky texture of rice noodles is an important backdrop
to the pungent flavors of the kim chee.*

1 teaspoon canola or
  vegetable oil
2 cups shredded white or
  regular cabbage
⅔ cup roughly chopped kim
  chee
¼ cup vegetable broth
1½ teaspoons dark brown sugar
8 ounces wide, flat rice noodles,
  soaked for 10 minutes in
  boiling water
½ cup diced red bell pepper
½ cup diced yellow bell pepper
2 teaspoons toasted sesame
  seeds (see Helpful Hint,
  page 24)
Soy sauce

In a large wok or skillet, heat the oil over medium heat. Stir-fry the cabbage until it is almost golden brown, about 3 minutes. Add the kim chee, broth, and sugar and bring to a simmer. Reduce the heat to medium-low and cook for 3 minutes. Drain the noodles, add them to the broth mixture, and cook until tender, about 3 minutes. Stir in the peppers.

Transfer to serving bowls and sprinkle with the sesame seeds. Serve with soy sauce on the side and, for true pickle lovers, additional kim chee.

Makes 6 servings

Per Serving:
167 Calories; 1g Protein; 1g Fat;
38g Carbohydrates; 0 Cholesterol;
162mg Sodium; 1g Fiber.

Mushroom Stew

½ ounce dried shiitake or
Chinese dried black mush-
rooms, soaked in 2 cups
water until soft (about
30 minutes)

1 tablespoon mild brown
bean sauce

2 tablespoons rice wine

2 tablespoons dark soy sauce

2 teaspoons canola or
vegetable oil

2 teaspoons minced garlic

1 tablespoon minced fresh
gingerroot

2 small shallots, peeled and
chopped (about ¾ cup)

8 ounces fresh wild or button
mushrooms, stemmed and
roughly chopped

Freshly ground black pepper

1 teaspoon sesame oil

3 tablespoons minced Chinese
chives, garlic chives, or
regular chives

6 cups cooked wide wheat
noodles (such as udon or
fettuccine), hot

1 bunch enoki mushrooms

Drain the mushrooms, reserving the liquid. Squeeze with your hands to remove excess liquid. Chop the mushrooms and set aside.

Pour 1 cup of the mushroom soaking liquid into a small bowl. (Be careful not to pour in any sediment or dirt that may have gathered in the bottom of the soaking bowl.) Stir in the bean sauce, rice wine, and soy sauce.

In a wok or skillet, heat the oil over medium-high heat. Stir-fry the garlic and ginger until fragrant, about 30 seconds. Add the shallots and stir-fry until light brown, about 2 minutes. Pour in the bean sauce mixture, reduce the heat to medium-low, and simmer, covered, for 5 minutes.

Increase the heat to medium and add all of the mushrooms except the enoki. Season with the pepper. Stir-fry until most of the liquid has been absorbed and the mushrooms are soft, about 2 minutes. Remove from the heat and stir in the sesame oil and 2 tablespoons of the chives. To serve, divide the noodles among 6 serving dishes and top with the mushroom mixture and sauce. Garnish with enoki mushrooms and the remaining chives.

Makes 6 servings

Per Serving:
251 Calories; 10g Protein; 4g Fat;
45g Carbohydrates; 0 Cholesterol;
872mg Sodium; 3g Fiber.

Singapore Noodles

This noodle dish is a favorite in restaurants and in homes throughout Singapore. This is a flavorful yet light and easy version.

⅓ cup vegetable broth

¼ cup coconut milk

2 tablespoons soy sauce

2½ teaspoons curry powder, or to taste

¼ cup chopped scallions

½ teaspoon freshly ground black pepper

1½ teaspoons canola or vegetable oil

2 teaspoons minced garlic

1 tablespoon minced gingerroot

1 small hot green chili pepper, minced (seeding is optional)

4 ounces firm tofu (1 cup), cut into ½-inch cubes

One 3-ounce can seasoned seitan, sliced into slivers (about 1 cup)

1 cup mung bean sprouts

2 cups spinach leaves

6 ounces rice vermicelli, soaked in warm water for 20 minutes and drained

1 tablespoon toasted coconut shreds (see Helpful Hint, page 88)

Spicy Tomato Sambal (page 54)

In a small bowl, mix together the broth, coconut milk, soy sauce, curry, scallions, and black pepper. Set aside.

In a large wok or skillet, heat the oil over medium-high heat. Stir-fry the garlic, ginger, and chili until fragrant, about 10 seconds. Add the tofu and seitan and stir-fry for 1 minute. Stir in the soy sauce mixture and bring to a simmer. Add ½ cup of the bean sprouts, spinach, and noodles. Stir-fry until thoroughly mixed.

Add the remaining sprouts. Serve in individual serving bowls or in a large serving bowl, and sprinkle with the coconut. Serve with sambal on the side.

Makes 4 to 6 servings

Per Serving:
423 Calories; 27g Protein; 13g Fat; 49g Carbohydrates; 0 Cholesterol; 702mg Sodium; 7g Fiber.

Helpful Hint

To toast coconut, preheat the oven to 375°F. Place coconut on a baking sheet and bake until light brown, about 10 minutes. Toasted coconut keeps well in a covered container, so don't hesitate to toast a few cups at a time to have on hand.

VARIATION

If desired, add egg strips to the stir-fry right before serving. Heat ½ teaspoon of canola or vegetable oil over medium-high heat in a 10-inch skillet. Pour in one large, lightly beaten egg and tilt the pan to form a thin sheet. Cook the egg until set, about 30 seconds. Gently turn over and lightly brown the other side. Remove from the heat and cool slightly. Roll it up and slice crosswise into thin strips.

Winter Soba

This dish is not only nutritious and easy, but also beautiful in the bowl.

**6 dried shiitake mushrooms
    (½ ounce), soaked until soft
    (about 30 minutes)**
8 ounces dried soba
2 tablespoons dark soy sauce
2 tablespoons lemon juice
1 cup vegetable broth
⅓ cup rice wine
**8 ounces red potatoes, cut into
    ½-inch pieces (1¾ cups)**
**1 medium onion, sliced into
    thin rings (1¼ cups)**
**4 ounces firm tofu, cut into
    ½-inch cubes (optional)**
1 cup shiso or spinach leaves
**½ medium daikon radish,
    peeled and cut into ½-inch
    pieces (1 cup)**
¼ cup chopped scallions
**1 teaspoon gomashio or sesame
    seeds**
1 teaspoon sesame oil
Additional soy sauce

Drain the mushrooms. Remove the woody stems and discard; cut the caps into small slivers. Set aside.

Cook the noodles until tender according to package directions; drain and plunge into a bowl of cold water. Drain and set aside.

While the noodles cook, mix together the soy sauce and lemon juice in a cup or small bowl.

In a wok or medium soup pot, heat the broth and rice wine to a simmer. Add the potatoes and onion. Cover and simmer until the potatoes are just tender, 8 to 10 minutes. Stir in the mushrooms and tofu if desired. Then stir in the noodles, shiso, daikon, and scallions.

Pour in the soy sauce mixture and toss until heated through. Remove from the heat and drizzle in the sesame oil. Sprinkle with gomashio at the table. Garnish with soy sauce to taste.

Makes 6 servings

Per Serving:
250 Calories; 8g Protein; 3g Fat; 45g Carbohydrates; 0 Cholesterol; 546mg Sodium; 4g Fiber.

Thai One-Bowl Noodle Soup

This substantial soup makes a meal.

6 ounces lo mein or thin
    spaghetti
½ medium lemon grass stalk,
    peeled
6 cups vegetable broth
1 teaspoon Thai Green Curry
    Paste, prepared or
    homemade (page 41)
1 cup shredded white cabbage
2 cups coarsely chopped
    mushrooms
6 ounces firm tofu, cut into
    ½-inch cubes
2 cups mung bean sprouts
1 cup snow peas, stemmed and
    slivered
1 lime, cut into thin wedges
Soy sauce

In a large wok or soup pot, cook the noodles until just tender according to package directions. Drain and rinse in cold water; drain and set aside in a colander.

Flatten the lemon grass stalk with the side of a large knife, and add it to the wok or soup pot with the broth and curry. Simmer 5 minutes.

Add the cabbage and mushrooms and cook until the cabbage wilts, about 1 minute. Add the noodles and tofu and cook for 30 seconds. Just before removing the wok or pot from the heat, discard the lemon grass and toss in ½ cup of the sprouts and the peas. Ladle the soup into serving bowls and serve with lime, soy sauce, and the remaining sprouts as garnish.

Makes 6 substantial servings

Per Serving:
140 Calories; 9g Protein; 3g Fat;
22g Carbohydrates; 0 Cholesterol;
90mg Sodium; 3g Fiber.

Japanese Udon Stew

The Japanese love their stews and soups with more noodles than vegetables. But if you prefer more vegetables, reduce the amount of noodles to eight ounces.

12 ounces fresh udon or flat, medium wide dried wheat noodles

1 teaspoon each canola and sesame oil

1 cup peeled and sliced carrots, cut into ⅛-inch coins

½ medium daikon radish, peeled and sliced (¾ cup)

1 small sweet potato, peeled and diced (1 cup)

4 cups vegetable broth

2 tablespoons mirin or other sweet wine

2 tablespoons dark soy sauce

4 to 5 medium-large fresh shiitake mushrooms, stemmed and cut into slivers (1 cup)

4 ounces firm tofu, cut into ½-inch cubes

½ cup scallions, cut into 2-inch lengths

1 sheet nori, toasted and cut into thin strips (see Helpful Hint, page 4)

Cook the noodles until almost tender; drain in a colander. While the noodles cook, heat the oils in a large soup pot over medium heat. Add the carrots, daikon, and sweet potato. Stir to coat them with the oil, then cook for 2 minutes.

Add the broth, mirin, and soy sauce. Heat to a simmer and cook until the potato is almost tender, 5 to 7 minutes. Stir in the mushrooms and tofu and simmer for 5 minutes more. Add the noodles and scallions and cook until the noodles are tender, about 2 minutes. Serve the stew in large soup bowls, ladling some of the broth over each serving. Scatter the nori over the top of the stew.

Makes 6 servings

Per Serving:
311 Calories; 13g Protein; 4g Fat; 56g Carbohydrates; 0 Cholesterol; 950mg Sodium; 5g Fiber.

Wasabi Noodles

Wasabi is Japanese horseradish, available fresh, powdered, and as a paste.
It packs quite a punch in this noodle dish.

1 pound cooked soba, chilled
1½ tablespoons dried wasabi
  powder
4 teaspoons cold water
1½ tablespoons dark or
  white miso
⅓ cup sake
¾ teaspoon brown sugar
1½ tablespoons rice vinegar
1½ tablespoons mustard
  (any type)
½ cup chopped scallions
2 teaspoons white sesame seeds

If the noodles have stuck together, loosen them by placing them in a colander and running cool water over them. While they drain, prepare the sauce: In a large bowl, mix together the wasabi and water to form a paste. Mix in the miso and sake. Then add the sugar, vinegar, and mustard. Remove a scant ½ cup of the sauce and set aside.

Mix the noodles in the bowl with the remaining sauce. Set aside for 10 to 15 minutes for the flavors to develop. (For a very mellow flavor, allow to sit, covered, for up to 1 day in the refrigerator.) Transfer to individual bowls and top with the scallions and the sesame seeds. Serve the rest of the sauce on the side.

Makes 6 servings

Per Serving:
198 Calories; 9g Protein; 1g Fat;
37g Carbohydrates; 0 Cholesterol;
297mg Sodium; 0g Fiber.

Fox Noodles

KITSUNE UDON

*This noodle dish is typical of the
"less is more" elegance of Japanese cuisine.*

12 ounces soba
2 cups vegetable broth
2 tablespoons dark soy sauce
¼ cup sake
3 ounces prepared dried
aburage, cut into ¼-inch
strips
⅓ cup chopped scallions
1 tablespoon white sesame
seeds, or 2 teaspoons
prepared gomashio

Cook the noodles in boiling water according to package directions. While the noodles cook, heat the broth, soy sauce, and sake to a simmer in a saucepan. Add the aburage and simmer for 10 minutes.

When the noodles are just tender, drain and rinse with lukewarm water. Transfer to individual bowls and top with the aburage. Pour a little of the broth over each bowl and sprinkle with the scallions and sesame seeds.

Makes 6 servings

Per Serving:
306 Calories; 12g Protein; 6g Fat;
48g Carbohydrates; 0 Cholesterol;
410mg Sodium; 3g Fiber.

Red Curry Platter

10 ounces round rice vermicelli or spaghetti, soaked in boiling water for 15 minutes
1 teaspoon canola or vegetable oil
2 medium leeks, sliced into 1-inch pieces (1 cup)
2 teaspoons Thai red curry paste
½ teaspoon sugar
½ cup vegetable broth, plus more as needed to finish cooking noodles
3 small Thai keffir lime leaves
¼ cup coconut milk
1 tablespoon soy sauce
1 tablespoon minced fresh basil
1 bunch mustard greens, steamed and roughly chopped
6 ounces firm tofu, cut into 1-inch cubes
1½ cups fresh mung bean sprouts
One 3-ounce can bamboo shoots, drained
Condiments (optional): Additional soy sauce; 1 lime cut into thin wedges; 1 hot green chili pepper, thinly sliced; basil leaves; ½ cup chopped scallions

While the noodles are soaking, make the sauce. In a wok or skillet, heat the oil over medium-high heat. Stir-fry the leeks, curry, and sugar until the leeks are slightly softened, about 45 seconds.

Stir in the broth, lime leaves, and coconut milk and bring to a simmer. Drain the noodles and add them to the broth. Simmer until the noodles are soft and the sauce has thickened, about 2 minutes. Remove the lime leaves and stir in the soy sauce and basil. If the noodles are not tender, add a little more broth and continue to simmer until tender.

Place the hot noodles in the center of large serving platter. Place the greens, tofu, sprouts, and bamboo shoots around the noodles. Serve little bowls of any or all of the suggested condiments if desired.

Makes 6 servings

Per Serving:
312 Calories; 13g Protein; 6g Fat; 49g Carbohydrates; 0 Cholesterol; 217mg Sodium; 7g Fiber.

Udon with Simmered Tofu

**1 pound fresh, or 12 ounces
 dried udon noodles or
 spaghetti**
7 cups vegetable broth
1 teaspoon brown sugar
2 tablespoons dark soy sauce
5 tablespoons sake
**4½ ounces prepared dried
 aburage, cut in half**
**6 fresh shiitake mushrooms,
 cut into slivers**
¼ cup chopped scallions
**One 7-inch square nori, toasted
 and cut into small strips
 (see Helpful Hint, page 4)**
**Gomashio or sesame seeds
 (optional)**

Cook the noodles until tender according to package directions. While they are cooking, heat 1 cup of the broth with the sugar, soy sauce, and 2 tablespoons of the sake to a simmer in a small saucepan. Add the aburage and mushrooms and simmer 15 minutes. (The sauce will be somewhat syrupy.) Remove from the heat.

In a separate pot, bring the remaining broth and sake to a boil. Divide the noodles among 6 bowls and top each with a square of aburage and a few scallions. Pour hot broth in each bowl and scatter the nori strips and remaining scallions over the top. Garnish with gomashio if desired.

Makes 6 servings

VARIATION

*Add ½ to 1 cup additional chopped
vegetables in season to the soup.*

Per Serving:
367 Calories; 19g Protein; 6g Fat;
57g Carbohydrates; 0 Cholesterol;
977mg Sodium; 3g Fiber.

Spicy Sesame Soba for Summer

The Japanese rely heavily on wasabi powder (ground horseradish) rather than chili peppers when heat is called for. But use with caution— wasabi can be a real sinus-opener.

⅓ cup vegetable broth
2½ tablespoons Asian sesame sauce or tahini
1 teaspoon finely grated fresh gingerroot and juice
1 teaspoon wasabi powder mixed with 1 tablespoon water
2 tablespoons sweet sake
1 tablespoon dark soy sauce
1 teaspoon sesame oil
1 pound dried thin soba
1 large bunch scallions, cut into 3-inch pieces
2 ounces fresh daikon radish, onion, or radish sprouts, minced
One 7-inch square nori, toasted and cut into small strips (see Helpful Hint, page 4)
¼ cup grated daikon radish
¼ cup thinly sliced pickled ginger

In a medium bowl, mix together the broth, sesame sauce, ginger and juice, wasabi paste, sake, soy sauce and sesame oil. Set aside to allow flavors to develop.

Meanwhile, cook the noodles until tender according to package directions. When they are almost done, add the scallions and cook for 1 minute. Drain into a colander, rinse with cold water, and drain again. Place noodles and scallions in a large bowl. Add daikon and mix well. Divide among 6 bowls, making sure to put a few scallions on each portion. Top each bowl with a few nori strips. Serve the noodles with the sauce, grated radish, and pickled ginger alongside.

Makes 6 servings

Per Serving:
315 Calories; 8g Protein; 4g Fat; 60g Carbohydrates; 0 Cholesterol; 239mg Sodium; 5g Fiber.

Quick Asian Raviolis in Broth

This recipe freezes well. To cook, just pop the frozen raviolis in the bubbly broth until heated through, about 7 minutes.

1¼-inch piece fresh gingerroot
1 clove garlic
1 stalk lemon grass, peeled
6 cups vegetable broth
3½ ounces firm tofu (½ cup)
1 large egg white
1 teaspoon Pepper Salt
 (page 146)
1 tablespoon Chinese rice wine
 or dry sherry
1 tablespoon soy sauce
½ cup chopped, cooked spinach
 (or frozen, thawed, and
 squeezed)
¼ cup chopped scallions
36 wonton wrappers
¼ cup loosely packed cilantro
 leaves

Using the back of a knife, flatten the ginger, garlic, and lemon grass. Add them along with the broth to a soup pot and bring to a simmer.

Meanwhile, in a food processor or blender, process the tofu, egg white, Pepper Salt, rice wine, soy sauce, spinach, and scallions to a thick paste. (Do not puree.) Transfer to a bowl. (There should be 1 cup.)

Place 18 wonton wrappers on a flat surface and brush each with a little water to moisten. Place about one tablespoon of the tofu mixture in the center of the wrappers.

Moisten the remaining whole wrappers and place over the fillings on the other wrappers, pressing the edges of the squares together to seal and form the ravioli.

Simmer the ravioli in the broth until they are just tender, 3 to 5 minutes. (At first the ravioli might stick together in the broth; gently pull them apart with a wooden spoon as they firm up in the simmering broth.)

Serve the ravioli in the broth sprinkled with cilantro.

Per Serving:
209 Calories; 9g Protein; 2g Fat; 38g Carbohydrates; 4mg Cholesterol; 577mg Sodium; 1g Fiber.

Makes 6 servings

Rice Noodles in Coconut-Lime Broth

Rice noodles absorb flavors and broth like sponges. (If this soup is made ahead and reheated, you might need more broth to thin it.)

12 ounces flat dried rice noodles, soaked in hot water for 15 minutes
1 small red bell pepper, seeded and coarsely chopped
1 hot red chili pepper, seeded
2 teaspoons minced fresh gingerroot
½ teaspoon dried lemon grass
1 small onion, coarsely chopped (1 cup)
1 clove garlic
1 teaspoon paprika
5½ cups vegetable broth
1½ teaspoons canola or vegetable oil
2 medium Asian (Japanese) eggplants (8 ounces total) peeled and diced (1½ cups)
¼ cup coconut milk
2 tablespoons chopped shallots, optional
1 large lime, cut into small wedges
1 cup mung bean sprouts

While noodles are soaking, place the peppers, ginger, lemon grass, onion, garlic, paprika, and 2 tablespoons of the broth in a blender or food processor and blend to a paste.

In a large wok or pan, heat 1 teaspoon of the oil over medium-high heat. Fry the paste for 2 minutes. When it begins to simmer and bubble, stir in the eggplants, the remaining broth, and the coconut milk. Heat to a simmer and cook until the eggplant is just soft, about 5 minutes.

Meanwhile, drain the noodles. Add the noodles to the pan and boil until the noodles are cooked, about 2 minutes. Remove from the heat and let the soup sit for a few minutes. (The noodles will continue to absorb some of the broth.) Meanwhile, in a small pan, stir-fry the shallots in the remaining oil until brown. Serve the soup in bowls with lime wedges, sprouts, and fried shallots if desired.

Makes 6 servings

Per Serving:
276 Calories; 2g Protein; 3g Fat; 60g Carbohydrates; 0 Cholesterol; 106mg Sodium; 2g Fiber.

Thai Crisp-Fried Noodles with Mushrooms

*The Thai combination of basil and mint gives a wonderful flavor
to the woodsy mushrooms.*

1 teaspoon canola or
   vegetable oil
2 teaspoons minced garlic
4 ounces large button mushrooms, cut into thick slices
4 ounces fresh shiitake mushrooms (about 1 cup),
   stemmed
One 4-ounce summer squash,
   chopped (about 2 cups)
One 4-ounce zucchini, chopped
   (2 cups)
2 medium shallots, minced
   (⅓ cup)
1 tablespoon minced fresh mint
1 tablespoon minced fresh Thai
   or regular basil leaves
1 hot red chili pepper, seeded
   and minced
1 tablespoon lime juice
2 recipes Noodle Cake (page 70)
Thai or regular basil leaves
Thai chili sauce

In a large wok or skillet, heat the oil over medium-high heat. Stir-fry the garlic until fragrant, about 20 seconds. Add the mushrooms and cook until slightly softened, about 2 minutes. Add the squash, zucchini, shallots, mint, basil, and chili and stir-fry for 2 minutes. Add the lime juice and cook until the zucchini is tender, about 2 minutes.

Stir in 4 cups of the fried noodles and cook until softened, about 30 seconds. Remove from the heat. Place remaining noodles on a large platter and spoon the zucchini mixture over the noodles. Scatter a few basil leaves over the top to taste. Serve with a dish of Thai chili sauce.

Makes 8 servings

Per Serving:
139 Calories; 4g Protein; 6g Fat;
18g Carbohydrates; 15mg Cholesterol; 316mg Sodium; 1g Fiber.

Japanese Summer Soup Pot

This cold summer soup relies on the vegetable broth for much of its flavor. Select a brand you know is well seasoned, or, better yet, make your own.

1 pound dried soba
1 teaspoon sesame oil
One 10-ounce bag spinach leaves, or 1 large bunch, trimmed and washed
1 large seedless cucumber, peeled and thinly sliced
1 small jicama, peeled and diced (1 cup)
1 small Asian apple pear or firm regular pear, peeled, cored, and diced (1 cup)
½ small daikon radish, peeled and grated
6 cups well-seasoned vegetable broth, chilled
1½ tablespoons dried wasabi powder, mixed with 2½ tablespoons water
½ cup minced scallions

Cook the noodles until tender, according to package directions. Drain and rinse with cold water. Drain again, add the sesame oil, and toss well.

While the noodles are cooking, place the spinach in a large bowl and add boiling water to cover. Let sit until the spinach is wilted, about 3 minutes. Drain, rinse in cold water, and drain again. Squeeze the leaves with your hands to remove excess water. Chop the leaves and stems. Set aside. (Alternatively, see Helpful Hint.)

Divide the noodles among 6 deep soup bowls. Arrange the spinach, cucumber, jicama, apple pear, and daikon on top of the noodles. Pour the chilled broth over the noodles. Serve with small bowls of the wasabi mixture and the scallions.

Makes 6 servings

Helpful Hint

Alternatively, microwave an unopened 10-ounce bag of prewashed spinach for 3 minutes, then rinse in cold water, drain, and chop. (This method probably isn't done in the tiny villages of Japan, but it works perfectly.)

Per Serving:
369 Calories; 10g Protein; 3g Fat; 75g Carbohydrates; 0 Cholesterol; 168mg Sodium; 8g Fiber.

Tart Plum Ramen with Tempura Drops

Tempura drops are the "croutons" made with the batter leftover from making tempura. They garnish many Japanese soups and stews.

1 pound ramen, cooked according to package directions and drained
1 teaspoon sesame oil
6 cups vegetable broth
2 tablespoons sake
1 tablespoon soy sauce
½ teaspoon brown sugar
1 piece wakame, soaked for 15 minutes in hot water, drained and slivered
1 cup sliced bamboo shoots
2 small turnips, peeled and shredded (1 cup)
1 cup shredded carrot
½ seedless cucumber, peeled and thinly sliced
1 tablespoon umeboshi paste, or 2 umeboshi plums, minced

FOR THE TEMPURA DROPS

½ cup all-purpose white flour
½ cup ice water
½ teaspoon baking soda
1 teaspoon canola or vegetable oil

Place the noodles in a bowl and add the sesame oil; toss well.

In a medium saucepan, bring the broth, sake, soy sauce, and sugar to a simmer. Add the wakame, bamboo shoots, turnip, and carrot and simmer for 6 to 8 minutes.

Meanwhile, make the tempura drops. Mix together the flour, ice water, and baking soda into a lumpy batter in a small bowl. In a medium nonstick skillet or on a griddle, heat the oil over medium heat. Using a chop stick or ½ teaspoon measure, dot the pan with little mounds of batter. Brown for about 1 minute on each side. You should have 24 tempura drops.

Divide the noodles among 6 bowls and top with the broth, vegetables, and tempura drops. Add some cucumber slices and a dollop of the plum paste.

Makes 6 servings

Per Serving (soup):
153 Calories; 4g Protein; 4g Fat; 26g Carbohydrates; 12mg Cholesterol; 878mg Sodium; 3g Fiber.

Per Serving (tempura drops):
11 Calories; 0g Protein; 0g Fat; 2g Carbohydrates; 0 Cholesterol; 26mg Sodium; 0g Fiber.

Thai Festival Yam

In Thailand, "yam" means salad, usually a main course salad.

¼ cup distilled white vinegar
2 tablespoons light soy sauce
1 tablespoon lime juice
2 teaspoons minced garlic
2 teaspoons canola or
      vegetable oil
1 red hot chili pepper, seeded
      and minced
1 teaspoon brown sugar
One 2-ounce package bean
      thread noodles, soaked in
      warm water for 5 minutes
1 cup mung bean sprouts
2 cups chopped, cooked green
      beans
1 medium cucumber, peeled,
      seeded, and chopped (1 cup)
1 tablespoon minced fresh mint
½ cup finely chopped red
      radishes
One 10-ounce bag spinach
      leaves, or 1 medium bunch,
      lightly steamed and
      chopped
Cilantro sprigs
Egg strips (see Variation,
      page 88), optional
Zest of 1 small lime

In a large bowl, mix together the vinegar, soy sauce, lime juice, garlic, oil, chili, and sugar. Set aside.

Bring a pot of water to a boil. Meanwhile, drain the noodles and cut into 3-inch lengths with scissors. Cook in the boiling water until they are transparent and glassy, about 30 seconds. Drain immediately and add to the soy sauce mixture.

Stir in the sprouts, green beans, cucumber, mint, and radishes. Transfer to a serving platter.

With your hands, press the steamed spinach into a ball. Slice the round in half, then into 6 small wedges. Place these around the noodles. Sprinkle the cilantro, eggs if desired, and lime zest around the perimeter.

Makes 6 servings

Per Serving:
110 Calories; 5g Protein; 2g Fat;
21g Carbohydrates; 0 Cholesterol;
430mg Sodium; 5g Fiber.

Crunchy Szechuan Mushrooms

If you like full-flavored, spicy dishes with lots of texture, you'll love these mushrooms with "attitude."

3 Chinese dried black mush-rooms, soaked in warm water for 20 minutes
8 ounces button mushrooms, minced
1 tablespoon rice flour
1 tablespoon soy sauce
1 tablespoon Chinese rice wine or dry sherry
1 teaspoon canola or vegetable oil
2 teaspoons minced fresh gingerroot
1½ to 2 teaspoons chili paste with garlic
1 small carrot, shredded (½ cup)
½ small onion, minced (½ cup)
¼ cup vegetable broth
⅔ recipe Noodle Cake (page 70)
¾ cup chopped scallions
1 teaspoon sesame oil
Additional 3 cups fried rice noodles or 1 large head romaine lettuce, separated into leaves (optional)

Drain the mushrooms and squeeze to remove excess water. Remove the woody stems and discard; slice the mushrooms very thinly. Place them in a large bowl and mix them with the button mushrooms, flour, soy sauce, and wine.

In a wok or skillet, heat the oil over medium-high heat. Stir-fry the ginger and chili paste for 20 seconds. Add the carrot and onion and stir-fry for 45 seconds. Add the mushroom mixture and stir-fry until it forms a thick paste, about 3 minutes.

Add the broth and quickly bring to a boil. Add the fried rice noodles and scallions and stir to soften them. Remove from the heat and stir in the sesame oil. Serve on a platter of fried rice noodles or spoon the mixture into the center of a large platter. Surround with fresh romaine leaves.

Makes 6 servings

Per Serving:
90 Calories; 3g Protein; 4g Fat; 12g Carbohydrates; 5mg Cholesterol; 281mg Sodium; 2g Fiber.

Curried Mai Fun Stew

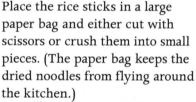

8 ounces mai fun noodles (thin rice sticks)
1 teaspoon canola or vegetable oil
½ small onion, minced (½ cup)
2 teaspoons minced fresh gingerroot
1½ teaspoons curry powder
1 stalk fresh lemon grass, peeled and minced
6 cups vegetable broth
2 tablespoons dark soy sauce
6 ounces firm tofu, cut into cubes
1 cup fresh peas or 1 cup frozen peas, thawed
Cilantro, mint, or basil sprigs

Place the rice sticks in a large paper bag and either cut with scissors or crush them into small pieces. (The paper bag keeps the dried noodles from flying around the kitchen.)

In a large wok or skillet, heat the oil over medium-high heat. Add the onion, ginger, curry, and lemon grass and stir-fry for 30 seconds. Add the rice sticks and stir-fry for 30 seconds.

Add 4 cups of the broth and bring to a simmer over medium-low heat. After the broth has evaporated and the noodles have slightly swelled, add another 1½ cups broth and cook just until the noodles are soft, about 30 seconds. Transfer the noodle mixture into a large, deep bowl.

Return the pot to the heat and bring the remaining ½ cup broth and soy sauce to a simmer. Place the tofu and peas in the broth mixture and simmer just until heated through. Pour the mixture with the liquid over the noodles. Garnish with the cilantro, mint, or basil.

Makes 6 servings

Per Serving:
144 Calories; 10g Protein; 7g Fat; 15g Carbohydrates; 0 Cholesterol; 1,467mg Sodium; 3g Fiber.

Miso-Root Vegetable Stew

8 cups vegetable broth
2 tablespoons soy sauce
2 teaspoons minced garlic
1½ teaspoons white miso
**3 medium turnips, peeled and
  cut into 1-inch cubes**
**1 small sweet potato, peeled
  and cut into 1-inch cubes**
**6 shiitake mushrooms,
  thinly sliced**
2 cups broccoli florets
2 cups shredded napa cabbage
**6 ounces firm tofu, cut into
  1-inch cubes**
**12 ounces cooked udon or
  spaghetti**

In a large soup pot, bring the broth, soy sauce, garlic, and miso to a simmer. Add the turnips and sweet potato, cover, and simmer for 5 minutes. Add the mushrooms and broccoli and cook until the broccoli is almost tender, about 5 minutes. Add the cabbage and tofu and simmer for 3 minutes.

While the vegetables are simmering, place the noodles in a colander and pour very hot tap water over them. Divide them among 6 large, deep soup bowls. Then ladle the vegetables and some of the broth over the noodles.

Makes 6 servings

Per Serving:
321 Calories; 18g Protein; 5g Fat;
57g Carbohydrates; 0 Cholesterol;
2,259mg Sodium; 5g Fiber.

Spicy Green Curry Noodles with Snow Peas

1 cup trimmed snow peas
8 ounces thin rice noodles
2 teaspoons canola or
vegetable oil
1 tablespoon Thai Green Curry
Paste, prepared or
homemade (page 41)
¾ cup chopped scallions, cut
into 2-inch lengths
7 ounces firm tofu, cut into
¾-inch cubes
½ cup vegetable broth
1 teaspoon brown sugar
2 tablespoons soy sauce

2 tablespoons minced cilantro

Place the peas and noodles in separate bowls. Pour boiling water to cover in each bowl. Let sit for 15 minutes; drain.

In a large wok or skillet, heat the oil over medium-high heat. Stir-fry the curry paste until fragrant, about 10 seconds. Add the scallions and stir-fry for 30 seconds. Add the tofu and stir-fry for about 2 minutes, taking care not to break up the cubes.

Add the peas and noodles and stir-fry for 30 seconds. Stir in the broth, sugar, and soy sauce and cook until the noodles are heated through, about 1 minute. Stir in the cilantro.

Makes 6 servings

Per Serving:
212 Calories; 6g Protein; 4g Fat;
38g Carbohydrates; 0 Cholesterol;
361mg Sodium; 2g Fiber.

CHAPTER 5

Main Dishes: Tofu

Asian Tofu Patties

7 ounces firm tofu

1 teaspoon chili paste
with garlic

2 teaspoons peeled and minced
fresh gingerroot

⅓ cup minced scallions

1 cup fresh whole grain or
white bread crumbs

2 large egg whites

1 tablespoon minced
cilantro leaves

½ cup chopped water chestnuts

2 tablespoons soy sauce

2 teaspoons canola or
vegetable oil

Hoisin sauce, Spicy Tomato
Sambal (page 54), or Chi-
nese chili sauce

In a medium bowl, mix together all of the ingredients except the oil and hoisin sauce. Mash to a chunky paste.

In a large nonstick skillet, heat the oil. Using a ½-cup measure, scoop the mixture into the pan and form into 4-inch patties. (Moisten your hands if the mixture seems too sticky.) Brown over medium heat, about 2 minutes. Reduce the heat to medium-low, turn the patties over, and brown the other side, cooking until the patties are cooked through, about 4 minutes. Serve hot with a dish of hoisin, sambal, or chili sauce.

Makes 4 servings

VARIATIONS

For appetizers, use a ¼-cup measure for smaller patties.

Instead of frying, bake the patties at 400°F for about 10 minutes per side.

Per Serving:
120 Calories; 8g Protein; 5g Fat;
11g Carbohydrates; 0 Cholesterol;
609mg Sodium; 2g Fiber.

Steamed Vegetables and Tofu with Spicy Coconut Sambal

Freshly grated coconut is well worth the effort here if you're fortunate to find one in your market. Otherwise, substitute unsweetened, dried coconut.

FOR THE SAMBAL

¾ cup freshly grated coconut
    or unsweetened dried chips
    or flakes
2 tablespoons lime juice
1 to 2 green or red hot chili
    peppers, seeded and
    minced
2 teaspoons minced garlic
1½ teaspoons brown sugar
Pinch of salt

FOR THE VEGETABLES AND TOFU

½ small white cabbage, cored
    and cut into 6 wedges
6 small new potatoes
2 medium turnips (about
    8 ounces), peeled and
    quartered
2 medium carrots, cut into
    3-inch pieces
1 pound firm tofu, cut into
    2-inch cubes

To prepare the sambal, mix together all of the ingredients in a small bowl and set aside.

In a steamer, steam the vegetables until just tender. Add the tofu and steam until heated through, about 5 minutes more.

Transfer vegetables and tofu to a large serving platter. Spoon sambal over them. Serve immediately.

Makes 6 servings

Per Serving:
162 Calories; 9g Protein; 6g Fat;
18g Carbohydrates; 0 Cholesterol;
171mg Sodium; 2g Fiber.

Kung Pao Tofu

*This classic peanut-flavored dish is lower in fat than the
restaurant variety, but not lower in flavor.*

¼ **cup raw peanuts, shelled
and skinned**
1 **tablespoon hoisin sauce**
¾ **cup vegetable broth**
⅓ **cup rice wine or dry sherry**
⅔ **cup rice flour**
½ **teaspoon salt**
1 **pound firm tofu, cut into
1-inch cubes**
2 **teaspoons canola oil**
1 **medium onion, cut into
slivers**
2 **teaspoons minced garlic**
1 **tablespoon minced fresh
gingerroot**
¼ **teaspoon red pepper flakes**
1 **cup chopped scallions**
½ **large green bell pepper,
julienned**
1 **teaspoon sesame oil**
4 **cups cooked rice, hot**

In a large wok or skillet, heat the
peanuts over medium-high heat.
Stir-fry them for about 3 minutes,
being very careful not to burn
them. Transfer to a plate and
set aside.

In a separate bowl, mix together the hoisin, broth, and
wine, and set aside.

Mix the rice flour and salt in a
large bowl and gently toss the tofu
cubes in the mixture with a

rubber scraper. Heat 1 teaspoon of
the oil in the pan over medium
heat. Add the tofu in one layer,
and let brown on one side. After it
stiffens, gently stir-fry to lightly
brown on all sides. Remove from
the heat and place on a plate.

Then add the remaining 1 teaspoon of oil to the pan and stir-fry
the onion, garlic, ginger, pepper
flakes, and ½ cup of the scallions.
Stir-fry this over medium heat
until the onion slightly softens,
about 1 minute. Add the bell
pepper and stir-fry for 30 seconds.

Add the broth mixture and cook
over medium-low heat, 2 to 3
minutes. Increase the heat to
medium-high and return the tofu
to the pan. Cook until the tofu is
heated through. (The sauce will
thicken and coat the vegetables
and tofu.) Drizzle on the sesame oil
and gently stir in the peanuts.
Remove from the heat and sprinkle
the remaining scallions on top.
Serve immediately with rice.

Makes 8 servings

Per Serving:
285 Calories; 14g Protein; 9g Fat;
39g Carbohydrates; 0 Cholesterol;
381mg Sodium; 3g Fiber.

Moo Shu Vegetables

7 ounces firm tofu

¼ cup rice flour

1 teaspoon canola or
    vegetable oil

2 teaspoons minced garlic

¼ teaspoon red pepper flakes

1 cup chopped scallions

½ cup sliced water chestnuts

½ cup chopped bamboo shoots

½ medium sweet red bell
    pepper, cut into ¼-inch
    strips, then into ¼-inch
    pieces (½ cup)

Egg strips (see Variation,
    page 88)

1 cup mung bean sprouts

2 tablespoons hoisin sauce

¼ cup vegetable broth

1 teaspoon sesame oil

Eight 6-inch mandarin
    pancakes or thin flour
    tortillas, warmed

Additional hoisin sauce

Place the tofu in a medium bowl and toss with the rice flour; set aside.

Heat the oil in a skillet and stir-fry the garlic and pepper flakes until fragrant, about 20 seconds. Add the tofu and stir-fry until lightly golden, about 3 minutes. (It will break up a little.) Then add the scallions, water chestnuts, bamboo shoots, and bell pepper; stir-fry 1 minute. Add the egg strips and sprouts and stir-fry until well mixed.

Add the hoisin sauce, broth, and sesame oil and stir-fry until most of the juices have evaporated, about 1 minute. Transfer the tofu mixture to a serving bowl, and serve with the warmed pancakes and hoisin sauce on the side. Diners should scoop about ½ cup of the tofu mixture onto the pancake, garnish with hoisin, and roll up like a burrito.

**Makes 8 servings
(about 4 cups)**

Per Serving:
113 Calories; 5g Protein; 3g Fat; 18g Carbohydrates; 26mg Cholesterol; 27mg Sodium; 2g Fiber.

Steamed Tofu with Corn, Black Beans, and Ginger Threads

This protein-packed dish is surprisingly light and refreshing, thanks to thin slivers of ginger.

14 ounces firm tofu, drained and cut crosswise into 4 rectangles
1 tablespoon minced fermented black beans
1 tablespoon peeled and slivered fresh gingerroot
¾ cup fresh or frozen corn kernels
1 teaspoon dark sesame oil
2 cups cooked rice, hot
Hoisin sauce, chili sauce, or Spicy Tomato Sambal (page 54)

Place the tofu squares in a steamer. Scatter the black beans, ginger, and corn over the top. Steam until the tofu is heated through, 7 to 10 minutes. Gently lift the tofu squares out of the steamer. Place on a serving plate and drizzle with oil. Serve the tofu hot with rice and any of the suggested condiments.

Makes 4 servings

Per Serving:
227 Calories; 13g Protein; 5g Fat; 31g Carbohydrates; 0 Cholesterol; 14mg Sodium; 1g Fiber.

Broiled Tofu with Sweet Soy Glaze

This tangy-sweet tofu dish is great with a simple salad and/or sliced daikon radishes and cucumbers as a crunchy garnish or side dish.

½ cup shoyu (Japanese
　soy sauce)
½ cup sake
2 tablespoons honey
14 ounces firm tofu, drained,
　cut crosswise into
　4 rectangles
2 cups cooked rice, hot

Preheat the broiler. Lightly oil a 9-inch baking pan. In a small saucepan, heat the shoyu, sake, and honey to a simmer. Cook until slightly syrupy, about 5 minutes. Remove from the heat and let cool for 5 minutes.

Place the tofu slices in the prepared pan and brush with the soy sauce mixture. Broil until browned, 3 to 5 minutes. Remove from the broiler, gently turn the tofu over, and brush with the soy sauce mixture. Broil until the tofu is heated through and has a deep, mahogany-brown color, 3 to 4 minutes. Serve hot with rice and a small pitcher of the remaining glaze.

Makes 4 servings

Per Serving:
253 Calories; 11g Protein; 3g Fat;
38g Carbohydrates; 0 Cholesterol;
2,095mg Sodium; 1g Fiber.

Stuffed Cabbage Rolls with Spicy Mustard

In Bali and Java, this dish is called stuffed banana leaves. If you can find banana leaves, use them—they're a great conversation starter.

**3 Chinese dried black mush-
rooms, soaked for 30 min-
utes in warm water,
drained and squeezed dry**
**12 large leaves of savoy or
regular white cabbage**
**2 teaspoons canola or
vegetable oil**
1 small shallot, thinly sliced
**½ teaspoon Chinese five-spice
powder**
2 cups shredded napa cabbage
1 cup shredded carrots
2 cups cooked rice
¼ cup chopped scallions
2 tablespoons dark soy sauce
1 teaspoon sesame oil
6 ounces firm tofu, chopped

FOR THE SPICY MUSTARD

⅔ cup Dijon-style mustard
2 teaspoons sesame oil
1 teaspoon hot chili oil
2½ tablespoons rice vinegar
**1½ teaspoons grated fresh
gingerroot**
1 medium scallion, chopped
Cilantro sprigs

Remove the mushroom stems and discard; slice the mushrooms into slivers. Place the cabbage leaves in a large bowl and pour in boiling water to cover. Let stand until softened, about 5 minutes. Drain and rinse twice, and set aside.

In a large wok or skillet, heat the oil over medium-high heat. Stir-fry the shallot and five-spice powder until fragrant, about 15 seconds. Add the napa cabbage, carrots, and mushrooms. Stir-fry for 15 seconds. Add the rice and scallions and stir-fry for 30 seconds. Remove from the heat and stir in the soy sauce and sesame oil. Cool slightly, then add the tofu, mashing it in gently.

To fill the cabbage leaves, place ⅓ cup of the tofu mixture at one corner of the cabbage leaf. Roll up like an envelope and place in a bamboo or metal steamer. Steam until the cabbage is very soft, 7 to 10 minutes.

While the cabbage rolls steam, make the spicy mustard by mixing all of the ingredients except the cilantro in a small bowl.

Serve the cabbage rolls on a large platter with a dish of the mustard in the center. Garnish with the cilantro sprigs.

Makes 6 servings

Per Serving:
152 Calories; 6g Protein; 5g Fat;
21g Carbohydrates; 0 Cholesterol;
393mg Sodium; 2g Fiber.

Tamarind Tofu

*Tamarind, the pulp from the brown pod of the tamarind tree, has a sour,
fruity flavor you'll probably recognize from Indian chutneys. Tamarind
is used throughout Asia as a flavoring. It is available in
this country as a paste, concentrate, or powder.*

⅔ cup sweet rice flour
14 ounces firm tofu, cut into
    quarters and then in half
    lengthwise to form
    8 squares
1 tablespoon canola or
    vegetable oil
1 hot red chili pepper, very
    thinly sliced
1 tablespoon finely chopped
    roasted peanuts
1 tablespoon tamarind paste,
    soaked in ½ cup very hot
    water for 15 minutes
2 tablespoons dark soy sauce
1 tablespoon lime juice
1 teaspoon brown sugar
¼ cup chopped scallions

Place the flour in a small bowl and
gently dredge the tofu squares in
it. Place them on a baking sheet or
plate and set aside.

To make the tamarind dipping
sauce, mix 1 teaspoon of the oil
with all of the remaining ingredients in a bowl. Set aside.

In a large skillet, heat the
remaining oil over medium heat.
Add the tofu and cook until
browned on each side, about
3 minutes per side. Remove from
the pan and place on a serving
plate. Serve the tamarind dipping
sauce in a separate bowl.

Makes 4 servings

Per Serving:
192 Calories; 10g Protein; 8g Fat;
23g Carbohydrates; 0 Cholesterol;
780mg Sodium; 1g Fiber.

Ginger Tofu with Fresh Ginger and Daikon Sambal

Get a double punch of ginger in this crunchy tofu main dish.

⅔ cup rice flour

¾ teaspoon ground ginger

14 ounces firm tofu, cut into quarters, then in half lengthwise to form 8 squares

2 teaspoons canola or vegetable oil

½ medium daikon radish, peeled and shredded (about ¾ cup)

1 tablespoon minced fresh gingerroot

1 tablespoon rice vinegar

½ teaspoon brown sugar

½ hot green chili pepper, minced

2 tablespoons soy sauce

¼ cup plus 1 teaspoon minced fresh cilantro

1 tablespoon canola or vegetable oil

In a medium bowl, mix together the rice flour and ginger. Gently dredge the tofu squares in the mixture. Set aside on a flat baking sheet or plate.

To make the sambal, mix together all of the remaining ingredients using 1½ teaspoons of the oil in a separate bowl. Set aside.

Heat the remaining oil in a large skillet over medium heat. Add the tofu and cook until browned on each side, about 3 minutes per side. Transfer to a serving platter and top each square with a little of the sambal. Serve the remaining sambal on the side.

Makes 4 servings

Per Serving:
243 Calories; 13g Protein; 9g Fat; 25g Carbohydrates; 0 Cholesterol; 532mg Sodium; 2g Fiber.

Savory Japanese Tofu Omelet

This is a takeoff on the traditional Japanese omelet called tamago.
Serve as a light supper or a brunch dish.

1 large egg plus 2 large egg whites, lightly beaten
1 tablespoon dark soy sauce
2 teaspoons sesame oil
1 tablespoon rice flour
7 ounces firm or soft tofu
1 teaspoon canola or vegetable oil
½ cup shredded carrot
½ cup shredded daikon radish
1 cup chopped fresh spinach leaves
3 cups cooked rice, hot
Additional soy sauce

In a medium bowl, mix together the egg and egg whites, soy sauce, 1 teaspoon of the sesame oil, rice flour, and tofu. Mash the tofu until almost smooth (a few lumps are okay).

In a 10-inch nonstick skillet, heat the oil over medium heat. Stir-fry the carrot and daikon until softened, about 1 minute. Then stir in the spinach and cook until the spinach is wilted, 4 to 5 minutes.

Level the vegetables in the pan, pour in the tofu mixture, and reduce the heat to medium-low. Cover the pan and cook for 5 minutes. Gently lift the underside to see if the bottom has browned. The top should be almost cooked through. Continue cooking, uncovered, to brown the bottom thoroughly. Turn the omelet over and cook until the underside is browned, about 5 minutes. Drizzle with the remaining sesame oil. Serve hot or at room temperature, cut into wedges, with rice and soy sauce on the side.

Makes 6 servings

Per Serving:
186 Calories; 8g Protein; 5g Fat; 26g Carbohydrates; 35mg Cholesterol; 217mg Sodium; 1g Fiber.

Mushroom-Tofu Stir-Fry with Daikon

This is traditionally served in China during the winter, because ginger and daikon are believed to have warming qualities for the body and spirit.

2 tablespoons Chinese rice wine or dry sherry
2 tablespoons mushroom or regular soy sauce
1 teaspoon canola or vegetable oil
2 teaspoons minced fresh gingerroot
2 teaspoons minced garlic
2 medium shallots, thinly sliced (⅓ cup)
¼ teaspoon red pepper flakes
1 cup peeled and diced daikon radish
8 ounces button mushrooms, sliced
1 teaspoon Pepper Salt (page 146)
5 ounces soft tofu
1 cup water spinach, watercress, or chopped fresh spinach
1 teaspoon sesame oil
3 cups cooked rice, hot

In a cup, mix together the wine and soy sauce. Set aside.

In a large wok or skillet, heat the oil over medium-high heat. Stir-fry the ginger, garlic, shallots, and pepper flakes until the shallots have softened slightly, about 1 minute. Add the daikon and mushrooms, season with Pepper Salt, and continue to stir-fry until the mushrooms begin to soften, about 1 minute.

Add the tofu and mash it in as you continue to stir-fry until the mushrooms are cooked through, about 2 minutes more. Add the soy sauce mixture and stir-fry until the liquids have evaporated, about 30 seconds. Stir in the spinach and remove from the heat. Drizzle with sesame oil and serve over rice.

Makes 6 servings

VARIATION

Substitute the same amount of shredded jicama or fresh or canned water chestnuts for the daikon radish for a less pungent flavor.

Per Serving:
157 Calories; 5g Protein; 3g Fat; 27g Carbohydrates; 0 Cholesterol; 358mg Sodium; 1g Fiber.

Spiced Tofu and Napa Cabbage

*On every Chinese restaurant menu you'll find a
tofu-cabbage dish like this one.*

⅓ cup rice flour
8 ounces firm tofu, cut into
    1-inch cubes
2 to 3 teaspoons hot chili paste
    with garlic
2 teaspoons vegetable oil
1 teaspoon brown sugar
½ large head napa cabbage,
    shredded (10 cups)
¼ cup vegetable broth
Cilantro sprigs
3 cups cooked rice, hot

Place the rice flour in a medium bowl. Gently dredge the tofu in the flour. Set aside on a plate. Discard any remaining flour.

In a large wok or skillet (see Helpful Hint), heat the chili paste, oil, and sugar over medium heat. Stir until it is fragrant, about 15 seconds, then add the tofu and stir-fry to mix it with the spice paste. (Don't worry if it breaks up.) Then add the cabbage and stir-fry for 1 minute to coat it with the tofu spice paste.

Stir in the broth, reduce the heat to medium-low, cover, and cook for 5 minutes. Stir again and cook, uncovered, until the cabbage is soft, 3 to 4 minutes. Garnish with cilantro and serve with rice.

Makes 6 servings

Helpful Hint

A large skillet is very important here—before it cooks down, the cabbage has a lot of volume.

Per Serving:
214 Calories; 8g Protein; 4g Fat;
37g Carbohydrates; 0 Cholesterol;
68mg Sodium; 3g Fiber.

Spicy Lemon-Grilled Tofu Packets

*These are great fun to tackle at the table—when you open
the hot packets, a burst of lovely aromas escapes.*

**2 medium shallots, thinly sliced
(⅓ cup)**
**2 teaspoons minced fresh
gingerroot**
1 teaspoon minced garlic
**1 small, hot red chili pepper,
seeded and minced**
1 tablespoon lemon juice
**⅓ cup fresh, or 2 tablespoons
dried, unsweetened coco-
nut chips or shreds**
8 ounces soft or silken tofu
1 tablespoon rice flour
1 teaspoon minced fresh basil
1 teaspoon minced fresh mint
**Six 7-inch squares lightly oiled
foil**
**Spicy Mustard (page 114), Mint
Sambal (page 8), or soy
sauce**
3 cups cooked rice, hot

Prepare a bamboo or regular
vegetable steamer.

In a medium bowl, mix to-
gether all of the ingredients
except the Spicy Mustard and
cooked rice. Mash to form a
light paste.

Using a ⅓-cup measure, scoop
tofu mixture into the center of
each foil square and lightly roll
into a cylinder. Place the packets
into the steamer and cook until
firm, 5 to 7 minutes. Cool slightly,
then serve the packets at the table
with Spicy Mustard and rice.

Makes 6 servings

Per Serving:
158 Calories; 4g Protein; 3g Fat;
28g Carbohydrates; 0 Cholesterol;
55mg Sodium; 1g Fiber.

Malaysian Lemon Grass Curried Tofu

*This dish is a blessing for the summer gardener looking
for another way out of the zucchini–bell pepper dilemma. The mint leaves
are not just for garnish: They should be eaten (sparingly!) with
mouthfuls of rice and curry.*

**1 teaspoon canola or
vegetable oil**
**½ cup chopped scallions, cut
into ½-inch pieces**
**2 teaspoons minced fresh
gingerroot**
**1 small green hot chili pepper,
sliced into very thin rings**
1 teaspoon dried lemon grass
1 teaspoon black mustard seeds
½ teaspoon ground cumin
½ teaspoon turmeric
**3 to 4 stalks celery, sliced
diagonally (1½ cups)**
**1 medium zucchini, cut into
thin rounds (1 cup)**
¼ cup vegetable broth
¼ cup pineapple juice
**8 ounces firm tofu, cut into
½-inch cubes**
**1 cup fresh pineapple, cut into
½-inch cubes**
**½ small sweet red bell
pepper, cut into narrow,
2-inch strips**
1 cup mung bean sprouts
3 cups cooked rice, hot
6 mint sprigs

In a large wok or skillet, heat the
oil over medium-high heat. Stir-fry
the scallions, ginger, chili, lemon
grass, mustard seeds, cumin, and
turmeric for 45 seconds. Add the
celery and zucchini and stir-fry for
1 minute. Then add the broth and
juice and heat to a simmer.

Stir in the tofu, pineapple, and
bell pepper and cook until the
tofu and vegetables are heated
through, about 30 seconds.
Remove from the heat and stir in
the bean sprouts. Serve on a large
platter in the midst of a mound of
rice, or serve over or alongside
rice. Garnish with mint.

Makes 6 servings

Per Serving:
188 Calories; 7g Protein; 3g Fat;
33g Carbohydrates; 0 Cholesterol;
106mg Sodium; 2g Fiber.

121

Tofu Lemon Grass Saté

7 ounces firm tofu

3 commercially prepared, crisp rice cakes, crushed

1 medium shallot, minced (¼ cup)

1 teaspoon minced fresh gingerroot

1 teaspoon minced garlic

½ teaspoon commercially prepared sambal oelek or chili sauce

2 tablespoons unsweetened coconut chips or shreds

1 large egg

6 medium lemon grass stalks, peeled

Peanut-Lime Sauce (page 138), Mint Sambal (page 8), or Sweet and Sour Sambal (page 132)

Preheat the oven to 450°F. In a large bowl, mix together all of the ingredients except the lemon grass and garnishes. Using the lemon grass stalks as the saté sticks, form about ⅓ cup of the tofu mixture around 1 end of the stalk (so that it looks like a ball on the end of a stick). Do this until you've used all of the tofu mixture and all of the stalks. Place in a lightly oiled 9×13-inch baking pan and roast until lightly browned, 10 to 12 minutes. Serve warm or at room temperature with the sambals.

Alternatively, shape the tofu mixture into 1¼-inch balls and place on a lightly oiled baking sheet. Bake about 10 minutes. Cool slightly, and serve on skewers or long toothpicks. (This is just as tasty but not quite as dramatic or fragrant.)

Makes 6 servings

Per Serving:
79 Calories; 5g Protein; 3g Fat; 7g Carbohydrates; 35mg Cholesterol; 45mg Sodium; 0g Fiber.

Hot and Tangy Tofu

2 tablespoons red wine vinegar

2 tablespoons rice wine

1 tablespoon soy sauce

½ teaspoon brown sugar

1½ to 2 teaspoons chili paste with garlic

1½ cups vegetable broth

1 large baking potato (10 ounces), cut into ½-inch cubes (2 cups)

½ medium napa cabbage, cut lengthwise into quarters, then cut in half crosswise

1 tablespoon fermented bean curd

5 ounces firm tofu, cut into ½-inch cubes

6 ounces rice vermicelli, soaked in hot water for 15 minutes and drained

1 tablespoon minced cilantro

In a small bowl, mix together the vinegar, wine, soy sauce, and sugar. Set aside.

In a large wok or skillet, heat the chili paste and the broth to a simmer. Add the potato and simmer, covered, until almost tender, 8 to 10 minutes. Add the cabbage, bean curd, and soy sauce mixture. Stir-fry until the cabbage is wilted and most of the liquids have evaporated, about 2 minutes.

Stir in the tofu and noodles and stir-fry until all of the juices have evaporated and the potato is fully cooked. Sprinkle with cilantro.

Makes 6 servings

Per Serving:
189 Calories; 5g Protein; 1g Fat; 41g Carbohydrates; 0 Cholesterol; 558mg Sodium; 2g Fiber.

Crisp Tofu and Rice Platter

FOR THE TOFU AND RICE

4 cups cooked rice
1 sweet red bell pepper,
    chopped
1 fresh ripe mango, diced
1 cup fresh peas, cooked, or
    1 cup frozen and
    thawed peas
2 tablespoons lime juice
2 teaspoons canola or
    vegetable oil
1 teaspoon minced fresh mint
½ cup rice flour
¼ teaspoon freshly ground
    black pepper
6 ounces firm tofu, cut into
    ¼-inch rectangles
½ firm banana, thinly sliced
Mint leaves

FOR THE TAMARIND SAUCE

1 tablespoon tamarind paste,
    softened in ½ cup hot water
    for 15 minutes
⅓ cup pineapple juice
½ cup diced pineapple
½ cup diced banana
1 teaspoon dark brown sugar
1 teaspoon minced fresh mint
1 teaspoon canola or
    vegetable oil

To prepare the tofu and rice: In a large bowl, mix together the rice, bell pepper, mango, peas, lime juice, 1 teaspoon of the oil, and the mint.

In a small bowl, mix together the flour and pepper. Lightly dredge the tofu in the flour mixture. Set aside.

Prepare the tamarind sauce: Push the tamarind through a strainer to extract as much of the pulp as possible. Discard the seeds. Place the strained liquid in a small bowl, add the remaining sauce ingredients, and mix well.

In a large nonstick skillet, heat the remaining teaspoon of oil over medium-high heat. Brown both sides of the tofu until golden, 3 to 4 minutes on each side. Place the rice mixture in the center of a large platter and place the tofu rectangles on one side. Place the banana and additional mint leaves on the other side. Serve a bowl of the tamarind sauce on the side.

Makes 6 servings

Per Serving:
337 Calories; 10g Protein; 6g Fat; 63g Carbohydrates; 0 Cholesterol; 110mg Sodium; 5g Fiber.

Tofu with Creamy Bean Sprouts

This humble little dish has a remarkable sweet flavor.
The sauce can also be used on grilled tempeh, or served alongside
steamed vegetables. It is generally used as a condiment like a sambal.

¾ cup milk

¼ cup coconut milk

1 teaspoon minced garlic

1 teaspoon minced fresh
    gingerroot

1 small shallot, sliced
    (2 tablespoons)

½ teaspoon dried lemon grass

4 cups mung bean sprouts

14 ounces firm tofu, cut into
    2-inch cubes

3 cups cooked rice, hot

¼ cup minced scallions

In a medium saucepan, bring the milk and coconut milk to a simmer. Add the garlic, ginger, shallot, and lemon grass and simmer over low heat for 5 minutes. Stir in 3 cups of the sprouts and increase the heat to medium-low. Cook until the liquids have almost all evaporated and the sprouts look very creamy, 7 to 10 minutes.

While the sprouts are cooking, steam the tofu cubes in a bamboo or metal steamer until hot. Place the rice on a large serving platter. Place the tofu on the rice and then spoon the creamy sprouts over the top. Scatter the scallions around the rice and rim the platter with the remaining sprouts.

Makes 6 servings

Per Serving:
206 Calories; 110g Protein; 6g Fat; 30g Carbohydrates; 0 Cholesterol; 46mg Sodium; 2g Fiber.

CHAPTER 6

Main Dishes: Tempeh

Indonesian Green Bean and Tempeh Stir-Fry

TUMIS BUNCHIS

1 pound green beans, trimmed and cut diagonally into 2-inch pieces

8 ounces peeled baby carrots

2 teaspoons canola or vegetable oil

½ to ¾ teaspoon commercially prepared sambal oelek or 1 small hot green chili pepper with seeds, minced

2 teaspoons minced garlic

1 tablespoon minced gingerroot

1 tablespoon minced fermented black beans

2 medium shallots, thinly sliced

8 ounces regular or multigrain tempeh, cut into 1-inch cubes

⅔ cup vegetable broth

2 tablespoons soy sauce

2 tablespoons toasted, unsweetened, dried coconut shreds

3 cups cooked rice, hot

Additional sambal oelek (optional)

In a large saucepan, parboil the green beans and carrots for 3 minutes; drain, rinse in cold water, and set aside to drain in a colander.

In a large wok or skillet, heat the oil over medium-high heat. Stir in the sambal, garlic, ginger, black beans, and shallots and cook for 30 seconds. Stir in the tempeh, reduce the heat to medium, and stir-fry for 1 minute. (The tempeh should be well coated.)

Stir in the green beans, carrots, broth, and soy sauce. Reduce heat to medium-low and cook until the carrots are just crisp-tender and almost all of the liquid has evaporated, 3 to 4 minutes. Transfer to a serving bowl and sprinkle with the coconut. Serve with a bowl of rice and additional sambal if desired.

Makes 6 servings

Per Serving:
243 Calories; 11g Protein; 5g Fat; 42g Carbohydrates; 0 Cholesterol; 472mg Sodium; 6g Fiber.

Tempeh and Potato Patties

These are as close to veggie burgers as you'll get in Bali.
On Bali beaches, they're hawked as "Bali-burgers."

1 large red potato (8 ounces),
quartered
4 ounces tempeh, diced
2 tablespoons coconut milk
1 large egg, lightly beaten
1 small sweet yellow or red bell
pepper, diced (½ cup)
1 medium shallot, chopped
1 tablespoon minced fresh
gingerroot
1 teaspoon dried lemon grass
¼ teaspoon cayenne pepper
⅔ cup rice flour
2 teaspoons canola or
vegetable oil
Hoisin sauce, soy sauce,
Spicy Tomato Sambal
(page 54), or Sweet and
Sour Sambal (page 132),
optional

In a small saucepan, bring the potato and enough water to cover to a boil. Cover and boil until tender, 10 to 12 minutes. Drain and cool by rinsing it under cold water.

Meanwhile, in a medium mixing bowl, mix together the tempeh, coconut milk, egg, pepper, shallot, ginger, lemon grass, and cayenne.

Peel the potato and add to the tempeh mixture. Mash everything together with a fork to a chunky puree. Pour the rice flour onto a large plate. Using ⅓ cup of the mixture at a time, form patties and dredge them in the rice flour.

In a large nonstick skillet or griddle, heat the oil over medium-high heat. Fry the patties until golden brown on both sides, 2 to 3 minutes. Serve with hoisin, soy sauce, or the sambals if desired.

Makes 6 servings

Per Serving:
181 Calories; 7g Protein; 5g Fat; 27g Carbohydrates; 35mg Cholesterol; 14mg Sodium; 3g Fiber.

Javanese Stir-Fried Tempeh

The use of paprika to flavor tempeh dishes is unique to Java.

2 teaspoons canola or
vegetable oil
1 hot green chili pepper, seeded
and minced
½ teaspoon paprika
8 ounces regular or multigrain
tempeh, diced
1 pound green beans, trimmed
and cut into ½-inch pieces
(4 cups)
1 cup vegetable broth
1 teaspoon dark brown sugar
1 tablespoon soy sauce
1 cup finely chopped red
bell pepper
4 cups cooked rice or rice
noodles, hot

In a large wok or skillet, heat the oil over medium-high heat. Stir-fry the chili with the paprika until the chili is fragrant, about 20 seconds. Add the tempeh and stir-fry for 1 minute. Add the green beans and stir-fry for 30 seconds.

Stir in the broth, sugar, and soy sauce. Reduce the heat to medium-low, cover, and cook until the beans are crisp-tender, 3 to 5 minutes. Increase the heat to medium-high and stir in the bell pepper. Stir-fry until the liquid has evaporated and the pepper is crisp-tender, about 2 minutes. Serve with rice or noodles.

Makes 8 servings

Per Serving:
199 Calories; 10g Protein; 4g Fat;
33g Carbohydrates; 0 Cholesterol;
287mg Sodium; 5g Fiber.

Sweet and Sour Tempeh

This quick dish is at home with Western or Asian accompaniments.

8 ounces regular or multigrain tempeh
2 teaspoons hot chili with garlic sauce, or to taste
2 tablespoons vegetable broth
Sweet and Sour Sambal (page 132)

Preheat the oven to 400°F. Cut the tempeh into quarters. Then slice each quarter in half lengthwise, into 3 × ¼-inch squares. Place the squares in a lightly oiled or nonstick baking pan.

In a cup or small bowl, mix together the chili sauce with the vegetable broth. Lightly brush the tempeh with the chili sauce mixture. Roast the squares for 10 minutes. Turn the squares over and roast until brown and heated through, 8 to 10 minutes. Remove from the oven, set aside, and preheat broiler.

Meanwhile, make the Sweet and Sour Sambal.

Lightly brush the tempeh with the sambal and broil for 1 minute. Brush again and serve with extra sambal on the side.

Makes 4 servings

Per Serving:
113 Calories; 12g Protein; 5g Fat; 8g Carbohydrates; 0 Cholesterol; 31mg Sodium; 4g Fiber.

Sweet and Sour Sambal

*This sambal appears every day on every table
in Bali and Java. Use it at any meal. It will keep for
one week in the refrigerator.*

**1 small shallot, minced
(2 tablespoons)**
**3 tablespoons kecap manis, or
3 tablespoons soy sauce
mixed with 2 teaspoons
brown sugar**
2 tablespoons lemon juice
½ teaspoon hot chili oil

In a small bowl, mix together all
of the ingredients.

Makes about ½ cup

Per Tablespoon:
15 Calories; 0g Protein; 0g Fat;
3g Carbohydrates; 0 Cholesterol;
515mg Sodium; 0g Fiber.

Stir-Fried Tamarind Tempeh

This is a typical Balinese stir-fry, boasting layers of flavors: lime, tamarind, garlic, cumin, sugar, and chili pepper.

1½ tablespoons tamarind paste, soaked in ¾ cup water
2 teaspoons kecap manis, or 1 tablespoon soy sauce mixed with 1 teaspoon brown sugar
2 tablespoons minced cilantro
2 teaspoons canola or vegetable oil
1 small shallot, minced
1 teaspoon minced garlic
½ teaspoon ground cumin
½ teaspoon ground coriander
1 small green chili pepper, minced
8 ounces regular or multigrain tempeh, cut into matchsticks (2 cups)
About 3 medium stalks celery, cut into matchsticks (2 cups)
3 cups cooked rice, hot
Mint Sambal (page 8) or Spicy Tomato Sambal (page 54) (optional)

Strain the tamarind into a small bowl, and mix the juice with the kecap manis and half of the cilantro. Set aside.

In a large wok or skillet, heat the oil over medium-high heat. Stir-fry the shallot, garlic, cumin, coriander, and chili until fragrant, about 30 seconds. Stir-fry the tempeh and celery until the tempeh starts to brown, about 2 minutes.

Stir in the tamarind mixture, lower the heat to medium, and cook until the liquid has been absorbed, about 30 seconds. Serve with rice and additional sambal if desired.

Makes 6 servings

Per Serving:
206 Calories; 10g Protein; 5g Fat; 31g Carbohydrates; 0 Cholesterol; 326mg Sodium; 4g Fiber.

Five-Spice Tempeh Squares

**1 pound regular or multigrain
  tempeh**
1 clove garlic, halved
**1 tablespoon canola or
  vegetable oil**
**1 tablespoon Chinese five-spice
  powder**
**Winter Tomato Sambal
  (page 135)**

Preheat the oven to 400°F.

Slice the tempeh into 6 rectangles. Rub both sides of each rectangle with the cut garlic clove. Then brush lightly with oil. Sprinkle the 5-spice mixture on the squares and press into the tempeh so that it adheres.
Bake for 10 minutes.

Meanwhile, prepare the Winter Tomato Sambal.

Top each tempeh rectangle with about 1 tablespoon of the Sambal. Bake for 5 minutes. Serve immediately.

Makes 6 servings

Per Serving:
170 Calories; 16g Protein; 8g Fat;
10g Carbohydrates; 0 Cholesterol;
22mg Sodium; 6g Fiber.

Winter Tomato Sambal

About 15 cherry tomatoes,
    halved (1 cup)
½ small, hot green chili pepper,
    seeded and minced
½ teaspoon brown sugar
1 teaspoon minced garlic
2 tablespoons chopped
    scallions
Salt to taste
1 tablespoon lemon juice or
    to taste

In a small saucepan, heat the tomatoes, chili, sugar, and garlic over medium-low heat. Break up the tomatoes into pieces with a spoon. Cook until tomatoes are soft, about 5 minutes.

Stir in the scallions. Add salt and lemon juice to taste.

Makes about ¾ cup

Per Tablespoon:
5 Calories; 0g Protein; 0g Fat;
1g Carbohydrates; 0 Cholesterol;
11mg Sodium; 0g Fiber.

Quick Simmered Pickles and Tempeh

This spicy, pickled vegetable dish is crunchy with
macadamias and hearty with tempeh.

¼ cup macadamia nuts

1 teaspoon minced garlic

½ teaspoon powdered turmeric

½ teaspoon sugar

½ teaspoon ground coriander

5 tablespoons vegetable broth

½ small onion, coarsely
    chopped (about ½ cup)

1 hot green chili pepper, seeded
    and coarsely chopped

1 cup peeled baby carrots, cut
    in half lengthwise

1 small head cauliflowerets
    (2 cups)

3 tablespoons distilled white
    vinegar

8 ounces regular or multigrain
    tempeh, cut into 3 × ¼-inch
    matchsticks

1 cup sliced bamboo shoots

1 tablespoon minced cilantro
    leaves

3 cups cooked rice, hot

Bring a large pot of water to a boil. While the water is heating, place the nuts, garlic, turmeric, sugar, coriander, 2 tablespoons of the broth, onion, and chili in a blender or food processor and blend to a smooth paste. Set aside.

Boil the carrots and cauliflower for 3 minutes. Drain and set aside.

In a large nonstick skillet, heat the nut paste over medium-high heat. Cook for 2 minutes, then add the carrots and cauliflower and stir-fry to coat the vegetables. Stir in the vinegar and remaining broth and bring to a simmer. Add the tempeh and bamboo shoots. Simmer until the tempeh is warmed through and almost all of the liquid has evaporated. Remove from the heat and stir in the cilantro. Serve hot, at room temperature, or cool, and store for up to 3 days before serving chilled. Serve with the rice.

Makes 6 servings

Per Serving:
249 Calories; 12g Protein; 8g Fat;
35g Carbohydrates; 0 Cholesterol;
106mg Sodium; 7g Fiber.

Peanut and Tempeh Sauce for Soft Rice Noodles or Rice

8 ounces regular or multigrain tempeh, chopped
1 tablespoon lime juice
Zest of 1 lime
2 medium shallots, minced (⅓ cup)
2 teaspoons minced fresh gingerroot
1 teaspoon minced galangal (optional)
2 teaspoons canola or vegetable oil
One recipe Peanut-Lime Sauce (page 138)
2 cups rice noodles or rice, hot
Cilantro sprigs
1 small lime, cut into thin wedges

In a large bowl, mix together the tempeh, lime juice, lime zest, shallots, ginger, galangal, if desired, and 1 teaspoon of the oil. Let marinate for 15 minutes. Meanwhile, make the Peanut-Lime Sauce and set aside.

Heat the remaining teaspoon of oil in a large wok or skillet. Remove the tempeh from the marinade and cook in the wok or skillet until golden, 3 to 5 minutes. (Discard marinade or save for another use.) Place the noodles on a large platter and make a well in the center. Spoon the cooked tempeh into the well. Top with half of the Peanut-Lime Sauce and the cilantro sprigs. Serve the rest of the sauce on the side with the lime wedges.

Makes 4 servings

Per Serving:
380 Calories; 12g Protein; 7g Fat; 69g Carbohydrates; 0 Cholesterol; 7mg Sodium; 5g Fiber.

Peanut-Lime Sauce

*This sauce is versatile enough to use as a sambal with many
other satés, steamed dishes, and grilled foods.*

3 tablespoons lime juice
2 tablespoons chunky-style
    natural peanut butter
2½ tablespoons coconut milk
½ teaspoon brown sugar
1 medium scallion, minced
    (2 tablespoons)
1 hot green chili pepper, seeded
    and minced
1 small shallot, minced (about
    2 tablespoons)
2 to 3 tablespoons hot water

In a medium bowl, mix together
all of the ingredients except the
water. Gradually add the water,
stirring to get a smooth sauce. Let
sit for 5 minutes before using.

Makes ¾ cup

Per Tablespoon:
26 Calories; 1g Protein; 2g Fat;
2g Carbohydrates; 0 Cholesterol;
33mg Sodium; 0g Fiber.

"Good Fortune" Tempeh

1 teaspoon canola or
    vegetable oil
2 teaspoons minced fresh
    gingerroot
8 ounces regular or multigrain
    tempeh, diced
1 cup vegetable broth
2 tablespoons white rice
2 medium shallots, minced
¼ cup chopped scallions
1 tablespoon lime juice
2 tablespoons soy sauce
½ teaspoon hot pepper flakes
½ teaspoon brown sugar
6 large leaves Boston, Bibb, or
    round red or green leaf
    lettuce
Fresh mint sprigs
Chili sauce to taste (optional)

In a wok or skillet, heat the oil over medium-high heat. Stir-fry the ginger until fragrant, about 20 seconds. Add the tempeh and stir-fry until slightly brown, about 1 minute. Add the broth and cook over high heat until the liquid evaporates, 3 to 5 minutes. Place in a large bowl and cool slightly.

While the tempeh cools, heat the rice in a small skillet over medium heat until toasted and light golden brown, 3 to 5 minutes. Remove from the heat and place in a spice grinder. Grind the rice to a fine powder and add it to the tempeh along with all of the remaining ingredients except the lettuce, mint, and chili sauce. Pile the tempeh mixture into the lettuce leaves and top with the mint sprigs. Serve warm or at room temperature with chili sauce if desired.

Makes 6 servings

Per Serving:
96 Calories; 9g Protein; 4g Fat;
8g Carbohydrates; 0 Cholesterol;
510mg Sodium; 3g Fiber.

CHAPTER 7

Sides and Salads

Tart Spinach and Asparagus Salad

This Asian-flavored green salad has an intense flavor that is similar to a relish. It can be made up to three or four hours in advance and refrigerated until serving time.

4 to 6 cups shredded spinach (1 small bunch or about ½ of a 10-ounce bag)
2 tablespoons miso, any variety
1 tablespoon toasted sesame seeds (see Helpful Hint, page 24)
1 teaspoon brown sugar
1 tablespoon rice vinegar
2 tablespoons lemon juice
1 teaspoon soy sauce
½ cup chopped scallions
2 cups chopped and cooked asparagus spears

Place the spinach shreds in a large serving bowl. In a separate small bowl, mix together the miso, sesame seeds, sugar, vinegar, lemon juice, soy sauce, and scallions. Add the asparagus and toss well. Marinate for 10 to 15 minutes to develop flavors.

Pour asparagus mixture over the shredded spinach and toss well. Serve immediately.

Makes 6 servings

Helpful Hint

If preparing in advance, toss with the spinach just before serving.

Per Serving:
40 Calories; 3g Protein; 1g Fat; 6g Carbohydrates; 0 Cholesterol; 170mg Sodium; 2g Fiber.

Two-Banana Salad

*Actually, this recipe calls for three bananas.
The "Two-Banana" in the title refers to the popular fruit
and to the banana chili peppers.*

**About 3 bananas, thinly sliced
(1 pound)**
**½ cup sliced yellow banana
chili pepper, (or other hot
chili) plus 1 cup seeded
green bell pepper, cut into
thin strips**
2 tablespoons lime juice
Zest of 1 lime
**1 tablespoon tightly packed
chopped mint leaves**
1 tablespoon sugar
Pinch of salt
**1½ tablespoons minced roasted
peanuts**

In a serving bowl, mix together
the bananas and peppers. In a
separate small bowl, mix together
the lime juice, zest, mint, sugar,
and salt. Pour over the banana-
pepper mixture. Top with the
roasted peanuts.

Makes 6 servings

Per Serving:
97 Calories; 1g Protein; 2g Fat;
22g Carbohydrates; 0 Cholesterol;
58mg Sodium; 2g Fiber.

Marinated Bok Choy Salad

1 pound baby bok choy
1 medium shallot, thinly sliced
½ cup water chestnuts
2 tablespoons orange juice
2 teaspoons canola oil
1 tablespoon white or rice
vinegar
2 tablespoons soy sauce
2 tablespoons roughly chopped
mint leaves
½ teaspoon freshly ground
black pepper
Soy sauce (optional)

Bring a large pot of lightly salted water to a boil. Place the whole bok choy into the pot and boil until the leaves are wilted and the stems are crisp-tender, about 3 minutes. Remove the bok choy from the boiling water, drain, plunge immediately into ice water, and drain again. Slice each bok choy lengthwise into quarters, and place on a serving plate.

Scatter the shallot slices and water chestnuts over the bok choy. In a small bowl, mix together all of the remaining ingredients and pour over the salad. Marinate about 10 minutes before serving. This may also be refrigerated for a few hours before serving. Serve with a small pitcher of soy sauce if desired.

Makes 6 servings

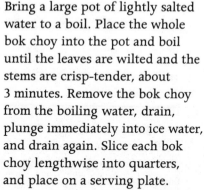

Per Serving:
37 Calories; 1g Protein; 2g Fat;
5g Carbohydrates; 0 Cholesterol;
409mg Sodium; 2g Fiber.

Quick Braised Asian Lettuces

The toasted peppercorns in the special Pepper Salt seasoning adds a mellowness to this unique side dish.

1 pound Asian salad mix (mixed Asian greens such as mizuna, mustard greens, and water spinach), or 2 heads soft leaf lettuce mixed with chopped young mustard or collard greens
1 teaspoon vegetable oil
2 teaspoons coarsely chopped fermented black beans
¾ cup chopped onion
1 large clove garlic, chopped
⅔ cup rice wine or dry sherry
1½ tablespoons soy sauce
1 teaspoon Pepper Salt (see page 146)

Place the greens in a large bowl. Pour boiling water over them. Let sit until wilted, 3 to 5 minutes. Drain, rinse with cold water, and drain again. Squeeze to remove excess water.

In a large wok or skillet, heat the oil over medium-high heat. Stir-fry the black beans and onion until the onion begins to soften, about 1 minute. Add the garlic and stir-fry for 15 seconds. Then add the lettuces and mix well.

Pour in the wine and soy sauce and reduce heat to medium-low. Cover and simmer until most of the moisture has been absorbed, 3 to 5 minutes. Sprinkle with the Pepper Salt and serve immediately.

Makes 6 servings

Per Serving:
59 Calories; 2g Protein; 1g Fat; 12g Carbohydrates; 0 Cholesterol; 515mg Sodium; 2g Fiber.

Pepper Salt

¼ cup salt
2 tablespoons Szechuan
peppercorns

Heat a small, heavy skillet over medium-high heat. Add the salt and peppercorns and toast, stirring occasionally, until the mixture is very fragrant, about 5 minutes. (The salt won't color but the peppercorns will get a shade darker.) Remove from the heat and let cool. Grind to a coarse powder in a spice or coffee grinder.

Makes about ⅓ cup

Helpful Hint

Pepper Salt will keep for months if stored in a tightly closed container, so be sure to make more than you need. (Several recipe in this cook-book call for Pepper Salt).

Per Teaspoon:
1 Calories; 0g Protein; 0g Fat;
0g Carbohydrates; 0 Cholesterol;
1,641mg Sodium; 0g Fiber.

Chinese Noodle Salad

*This side dish also makes a tasty, hearty addition
to a brown-bag lunch the next day.*

**9 ounces fresh vermicelli, angel
  hair pasta, or linguine,
  cooked**
2 tablespoons soy sauce
**1 tablespoon dark ("toasted")
  sesame oil**
1 teaspoon hot chili oil
**2 tablespoons black or
  balsamic vinegar**
1 teaspoon brown sugar
½ cup chopped scallions
½ cup mung bean sprouts

Place the noodles in a large
serving bowl. In a separate
medium bowl, mix together the
soy sauce, oils, vinegar, and sugar.
Pour mixture over the noodles and
toss well. Mix in the scallions and
bean sprouts. Let salad sit for at
least 10 minutes before serving.

Makes 6 servings

Per Serving:
190 Calories; 4g Protein; 6g Fat;
33g Carbohydrates; 0 Cholesterol;
422mg Sodium; 2g Fiber.

Corn and Cilantro Cakes

These flavorful and colorful cilantro-flavored corn pancakes can be served as a side dish or as a main dish, accompanied by a chutney or sambal.

1 cup cooked fresh corn kernels
    or 1 cup frozen and thawed
    corn kernels

1 medium shallot, chopped, or
    ⅓ cup chopped red onion

½ cup rice flour

2 tablespoons minced cilantro
    leaves

⅓ cup coconut milk

⅓ cup water

1 teaspoon baking powder

1 teaspoon salt

½ teaspoon turmeric

½ teaspoon freshly ground
    black pepper

¼ teaspoon cayenne pepper

2 teaspoons canola or
    vegetable oil

In a large bowl, mix together all of the ingredients except the oil.

Coat a nonstick griddle or skillet with the oil and heat over medium-high heat. Drop the corn batter by heaping tablespoons onto the griddle and cook until they are lightly browned on both sides, 2 to 3 minutes per side.

Makes 12 cakes, 6 servings

Per Serving:
57 Calories; 1g Protein; 2g Fat;
9g Carbohydrates; 0 Cholesterol;
229mg Sodium; 1g Fiber.

Cold Soba Salad

1 pound soba
¼ cup soy sauce
2 tablespoons lemon juice
¼ cup vegetable broth
¼ cup mirin or sweet
    white wine
1 tablespoon sesame oil
1 cup chopped scallions
Lemon wedges

Bring 4 quarts of water to a boil. Add the noodles and cook until tender, 6 to 8 minutes, or according to package instructions.

Meanwhile, mix together the soy sauce, lemon juice, broth, mirin, and oil in a small bowl.

When the noodles are done, drain them in a colander and plunge immediately into a bowl of ice water to chill them. Thoroughly drain the noodles again, and transfer them to a large serving bowl.

Pour the soy sauce mixture over the noodles and toss well to coat. Add the scallions and toss again. Serve in individual bowls with lemon wedges alongside.

Makes 8 servings

Per Serving:
237 Calories; 6g Protein; 3g Fat; 46g Carbohydrates; 0 Cholesterol; 648mg Sodium; 3g Fiber.

Miso-Braised Eggplant

This savory side dish has a silky smooth texture.

2 teaspoons canola or
    vegetable oil
1 large eggplant (1 pound),
    unpeeled and cut into
    ¾-inch cubes (about
    5½ cups)
⅔ cup vegetable broth
2 tablespoons dark miso
1 tablespoon honey
1 tablespoon rice vinegar
1 teaspoon sesame oil
¼ cup chopped scallions
    (green tops only), cut into
    ½-inch pieces

In a 10-inch nonstick skillet, heat the oil over medium-high heat. Add the eggplant cubes and cook until golden brown, about 5 minutes. Stir in the broth and reduce the heat to medium-low. Cover the pan and cook until the eggplant is tender, about 5 minutes. (The liquid will evaporate.)

While the eggplant cooks, blend together the miso, honey, vinegar, and sesame oil in a small bowl. When the eggplant is tender, stir in the miso mixture. Cook, stirring, until flavors are well blended, about 1 minute.

Transfer mixture to a serving bowl and cool slightly. Sprinkle with the scallions and serve warm or at room temperature.

Makes 4 servings

Per Serving:
90 Calories; 2g Protein; 4g Fat;
14g Carbohydrates; 0 Cholesterol;
292mg Sodium; 3g Fiber.

"Flying" Spinach

How do you make spinach fly? Thai legend tells of two chefs who used to toss spinach from wok to wok—while standing on opposite sides of the street. In legend, spinach really does fly.

Two 10-ounce packages spinach leaves, or 2 large bunches spinach
2 teaspoons canola or vegetable oil
1 tablespoon minced garlic
½ to 1 teaspoon chili bean sauce
⅓ cup rice wine or vegetable broth

Place the spinach in a large bowl. Pour in boiling water to cover and let sit until wilted, about 3 minutes. Drain, rinse in cold water, and drain again. Squeeze to remove excess water, and then roughly chop the dried leaves.

In a large wok or skillet, heat the oil over medium-high heat. Add the garlic and stir-fry until golden and fragrant, about 20 seconds. Add the chili bean sauce and stir-fry for 10 seconds. Add the spinach and stir-fry over medium heat for about 15 seconds more.

Splash in the wine. (It will evaporate almost immediately.) Continue stir-frying until the spinach is heated through. Toss and stir them quickly to avoid sticking. (This is the "flying" part.) Serve immediately.

Makes 6 servings

Per Serving:
50 Calories; 3g Protein; 2g Fat;
7g Carbohydrates; 0 Cholesterol;
198mg Sodium; 3g Fiber.

Green Bean Salad with Fried Shallots and Chilies

1 pound green beans, cooked until crisp-tender
1 tablespoon canola or vegetable oil
2 medium shallots, sliced into thin rings (about ⅓ cup)
2 tablespoons lime juice
1 medium hot green chili pepper, minced
2 tablespoons rice vinegar
1 teaspoon sesame oil
Soy sauce (optional)
Lime juice (optional)

Cut the beans into ½-inch pieces. In a medium wok or skillet, heat 1 teaspoon of the oil over medium heat. Add the shallots and stir-fry until they're well coated with the oil, then cook, stirring occasionally, until the shallots are golden brown, about 8 minutes. (They should be thoroughly browned but not burned.) Transfer them to a small bowl and set aside.

In a medium bowl, mix together the remaining oil, lime juice, chili, vinegar, and sesame oil. Mix in the beans and serve immediately, or chill the salad for up to 1 day before serving. To serve, sprinkle with shallots. Sprinkle with soy sauce and lime juice if desired.

Makes 6 servings

Helpful Hint

If you intend to chill the recipe for later, don't add the soy sauce until serving time; the beans tend to darken if the soy sauce is added before refrigeration.

Per Tablespoon:
54 Calories; 1g Protein; 3g Fat; 6g Carbohydrates; 0 Cholesterol; 221mg Sodium; 3g Fiber.

Stir-Fried Greens with Fermented Bean Sauce

*Most stir-fries lose their luster the next day,
but this one served cold will make a good lunch.*

**1 large bunch mustard, collard
  greens, or bok choy,
  washed and trimmed**
**1 tablespoon canola or
  vegetable oil**
**1 tablespoon minced fresh
  gingerroot**
**2 tablespoons fermented black
  bean sauce**
1 tablespoon soy sauce
**1 medium bunch scallions
  (about 7), trimmed and
  chopped (about 1 cup)**

Heat a large pot of lightly salted water to boiling. Add the greens and cook until the leaves are dark green and the stems are crisp-tender. Drain the greens, rinse in cold water, and drain again. Thoroughly pat dry and roughly chop the greens into 2-inch pieces.

In a large wok or skillet, heat the oil over medium heat. Add the ginger and stir-fry until fragrant, about 10 seconds. Add the greens and toss to coat lightly with the oil. Add the bean sauce and stir-fry, mashing in the sauce as you toss and heat the greens. Cook until the stems of the greens are still slightly crisp, 3 to 5 minutes. Sprinkle with the soy sauce, add the scallions, and stir-fry for 30 seconds. Serve immediately.

Makes 6 servings

Per Serving:
50 Calories; 3g Protein; 3g Fat;
4g Carbohydrates; 0 Cholesterol;
396mg Sodium; 2g Fiber.

153

Green Papaya Salad

1 large green (unripened)
    papaya, peeled, seeded, and
    cut into 1½-inch cubes
    (about 3 cups)
10 cherry tomatoes, halved
2 tablespoons very finely
    chopped roasted peanuts
1 teaspoon salt
½ teaspoon cayenne pepper
¼ teaspoon sugar
Lime wedges

Place the papaya cubes and tomatoes in a medium mixing bowl. In a separate smaller bowl, mix together the peanuts, salt, cayenne, and sugar; sprinkle over the fruit. Let salad marinate about 10 minutes before serving. Serve with lime wedges.

Makes 6 servings

VARIATION

Substitute a green mango for the green papaya, and chili powder for the cayenne.

Per Serving:
54 Calories; 1g Protein; 2g Fat;
10g Carbohydrates; 0 Cholesterol;
418mg Sodium; 2g Fiber.

Jicama, Mango, and Fresh Enoki Mushroom Salad

1 large ripe mango, peeled and
    cut into irregular 1-inch
    cubes (2 cups)
1 medium jicama, peeled and
    chopped into 1-inch cubes
    (1½ to 2 cups)
½ cup trimmed and diced red
    radishes
1 small hot chili pepper, seeded
    and minced
1 teaspoon raw brown sugar
½ teaspoon salt
2 teaspoons finely minced
    tender inner portion of a
    lemon grass stalk
2 tablespoons lime juice
Zest of 1 small lime
1½ ounces enoki mushrooms,
    separated
1 tablespoon tightly packed
    chopped mint leaves

In a large bowl, combine the mango, jicama, and radishes. In a separate bowl, mix together the chili, sugar, salt, lemon grass, and lime juice and zest; pour over the fruit. Mix half of the enoki mushrooms into the salad. Top the salad with the remaining mushrooms and mint leaves.

Makes 6 servings

Per Serving:
43 Calories; 1g Protein; 0g Fat;
11g Carbohydrates; 0 Cholesterol;
235mg Sodium; 2g Fiber.

Long-Bean Salad

This salad is especially good in summer when beans are garden-fresh.

3 cups cooked yard-long or
   regular green beans,
   chopped into 2-inch pieces
1 small onion, thinly sliced
   (½ cup)
2 tablespoons lemon juice
1 tablespoon chopped cilantro
1 tablespoon soy sauce
1 teaspoon canola or
   vegetable oil
2 teaspoons minced fresh
   gingerroot
2 teaspoons minced garlic
2 teaspoons sesame seeds
½ teaspoon hot chili oil

Place the chopped beans and onion in a medium bowl. Sprinkle with the lemon juice, cilantro, and soy sauce.

In a small skillet or wok, heat the oil over medium heat. Stir-fry the ginger, garlic, and sesame seeds until the mixture is fragrant and the sesame seeds begin to pop, about 30 seconds. Remove the pan from the heat and pour the sesame seed mixture over the vegetables. Sprinkle on the hot chili oil and toss the salad to mix well.

Makes 6 servings

Per Serving:
43 Calories; 2g Protein; 2g Fat;
7g Carbohydrates; 0 Cholesterol;
181mg Sodium; 3g Fiber.

Mixed Mushroom Salad

Any wild mushrooms—oyster, cremini, porcinis—can be substituted for the shiitakes in this salad.

2 teaspoons canola or
vegetable oil
2 teaspoons minced garlic
2 cups stemmed and halved
fresh shiitake mushrooms
About 8 ounces small button
mushrooms, stemmed
(2½ cups)
⅓ cup rice wine
Salt and freshly ground black
pepper
One 15-ounce can straw mushrooms, rinsed and drained
1 medium bunch minced
Chinese or regular chives
2 tablespoons fresh lime juice
Zest of 1 lime
2 tablespoons rice vinegar
1 tablespoon mushroom or
regular soy sauce
Shredded spinach leaves
½ tablespoon toasted sesame
seeds (see Helpful Hint,
page 24)

In a large wok or skillet, heat
1 teaspoon of the oil over medium
heat. Add the garlic and stir-fry
until fragrant, 15 to 20 seconds.
Add the shiitake and button
mushrooms and stir-fry for
1 minute. Add the wine and
reduce heat to medium-low.
Season lightly with salt and
pepper. Cook until the shiitake
mushrooms are soft, 3 to 5 minutes. Mix in the straw mushrooms
and chives and transfer to a bowl.

In a separate small bowl, stir
together the remaining teaspoon
of oil, lime juice, zest, vinegar,
and soy sauce; pour over the
mushroom mixture.

Place the spinach leaves on
individual plates or on a large
serving platter. Pile the mushrooms in the center and sprinkle
with sesame seeds.

Makes 6 servings

Per Serving:
84 Calories; 3g Protein; 2g Fat;
16g Carbohydrates; 0 Cholesterol;
301mg Sodium; 2g Fiber.

Summer Nut Salad

This refreshing salad can be used as a condiment or mixed with rice for a heartier dish.

⅓ cup chopped roasted cashews
1 tablespoon minced crystallized ginger
¼ cup loosely packed dried coconut chips
2 cups peeled and diced cucumber
1 small hot red chili pepper, seeded and minced
2 tablespoons lemon juice
1 tablespoon minced basil
½ teaspoon brown sugar
½ teaspoon salt
2 teaspoons canola or vegetable oil
1 teaspoon sesame seeds
¼ teaspoon cayenne pepper
3 cups cooked rice, at room temperature (optional)

In a medium bowl, mix together the cashews, ginger, coconut, cucumber, chili, lemon juice, basil, sugar, and salt.

In a small nonstick skillet, heat the oil over medium-high heat. Add the sesame seeds and stir-fry until they begin to darken and pop. Stir in the cayenne, remove the pan from the heat, and gently stir into the coconut mixture.

Set aside for 10 minutes before serving. (The cucumber will soften slightly.) Serve as a salad, or with rice, if desired, as a main dish.

Makes 6 servings

Per Serving:
90 Calories; 2g Protein; 6g Fat; 8g Carbohydrates; 0 Cholesterol; 236mg Sodium; 1g Fiber.

Pineapple, Cucumber, and Mung Bean Sprout Salad

1 medium pineapple, peeled,
cored, and chopped into
1½-inch cubes (about
3 cups)
1 medium cucumber, peeled,
seeded, and chopped into
1-inch pieces (about 1 cup)
8 ounces fresh mung bean
sprouts (about 3 cups)
1 to 2 hot green chili peppers,
seeded and minced, or
to taste
2 tablespoons lime juice
¼ to ½ teaspoon cayenne
pepper, or to taste
1 tablespoon canola or
vegetable oil
2 tablespoons pineapple juice
Pinch of salt
2 tablespoons fresh chopped
mint

Place the pineapple, cucumber, and bean sprouts in a large bowl. In a separate small mixing bowl, whisk together all of the remaining ingredients using 1 tablespoon of the mint. Add to the pineapple mixture and toss gently but thoroughly. Top with the remaining mint and serve immediately or refrigerate before serving.

Makes 6 to 8 servings

Per Serving:
84 Calories; 2g Protein; 3g Fat;
15g Carbohydrates; 0 Cholesterol;
43mg Sodium; 2g Fiber.

Mixed Japanese Radish Salad

½ **medium daikon radish,
cut into 1-inch cubes
(about 2 cups)**
7 **or 8 red radishes, thinly sliced
(1 cup)**
2 **teaspoons dark ("toasted")
sesame oil**
1 **teaspoon wasabi powder
mixed with 1 tablespoon
water**
2 **tablespoons lemon juice**
½ **tablespoon sesame seeds**
1 **tablespoon rice vinegar**
1 **teaspoon soy sauce**
½ **cup radish or onion sprouts**

Place daikon and red radishes in a
medium bowl. In a separate bowl,
mix together all of the remaining
ingredients except the sprouts.
Pour the dressing over the salad
and top with the sprouts.

Makes 6 servings

Per Serving:
29 Calories; 1g Protein; 2g Fat;
3g Carbohydrates; 0 Cholesterol;
65mg Sodium; 1g Fiber.

Indonesian Spiced Fruit Salad

RUJAK

*Indonesians eat this fruit salad almost every day,
either as a snack from street vendors or with rice, sambal,
and grilled foods as part of a large meal.*

1 tablespoon tamarind paste, or
   3 tablespoons lime juice
1 small cucumber, peeled,
   seeded, and chopped
   (¾ cup)
½ cup sliced water chestnuts
1 cup cubed pineapple (1-inch
   cubes)
1 small green apple, cut into
   1-inch pieces
1 small pear, cut into 1-inch
   pieces
1 firm banana, sliced into
   ⅓-inch rounds
1 hot chili pepper, seeded and
   minced
1 tablespoon brown sugar
Pinch of salt
2 tablespoons chopped toasted
   macadamia nuts

If using the tamarind paste, soak it in about ½ cup very hot water for 15 minutes. Pull the paste apart with your fingers to break it up. Put the paste back in the hot water. Drain, reserving the liquid. Discard the tamarind pulp.

Place the cucumber, water chestnuts, pineapple, apple, pear, and banana in a large serving bowl. In a separate smaller bowl, mix together the chili, tamarind liquid, brown sugar, and salt. Pour over the fruit and gently toss the mixture together to coat all of the fruit with the dressing. Sprinkle the macadamia nuts on top.

Makes 8 servings

Per Serving:
145 Calories; 1g Protein; 4g Fat;
30g Carbohydrates; 0 Cholesterol;
210mg Sodium; 4g Fiber.

Stir-Fried Spinach Crowns

**1 teaspoon canola or
vegetable oil**
2 teaspoons minced garlic
**2 teaspoons minced fresh
gingerroot**
**½ hot green chili pepper,
minced (about 1 teaspoon)**
**8 spinach "crowns" from
2 bunches of spinach
(about 8 ounces), cut in half
(see Helpful Hint)**
**1 tablespoon mushroom soy
sauce**
¼ cup vegetable broth
**1 tablespoon black vinegar or
balsamic vinegar**
1 teaspoon sesame oil
Soy sauce to taste (optional)

In a large wok or skillet, heat the
oil over medium-high heat. Add
the garlic, ginger, and chili and
stir-fry for 30 seconds. Add the
spinach and stir. Add the soy
sauce, broth, and vinegar and stir
to blend. Cover and simmer over
medium-low heat for 3 to 4 minutes. Remove the cover, and
increase the heat to medium; cook
until most of the juices have
evaporated, about 2 minutes.
Sprinkle with sesame oil and soy
sauce if desired, before serving.

Makes 4 to 6 servings

Helpful Hint

*Crowns are the bottom 3 to 4 inches
of the spinach plant, including the
base and bottom part of the stem.*

Per Serving:
30 Calories; 1g Protein; 2g Fat;
2g Carbohydrates; 0 Cholesterol;
342mg Sodium; 0g Fiber.

Stir-Fried Garlic Spinach

1 teaspoon canola or
   vegetable oil
1 tablespoon peeled fresh
   gingerroot, cut into
   ⅛ × 1-inch matchsticks
2 cloves garlic, sliced
2 large bunches spinach,
   trimmed at the base with
   tender stems attached
1½ teaspoons sesame oil
1 tablespoon soy sauce

In a large wok, heat the oil over medium-high heat. Add ginger and garlic and stir-fry until light brown, about 1 minute. Add the spinach and toss (as if you were tossing a salad) until wilted, about 1 minute, making sure to toss the garlic and ginger so that they don't burn. Drizzle with sesame oil and soy sauce and serve immediately.

Makes 4 to 6 servings

Per Serving:
68 Calories; 5g Protein; 3g Fat;
7g Carbohydrates; 0 Cholesterol;
390mg Sodium; 5g Fiber.

Sweet and Sour Red Cabbage Slaw

½ **medium red cabbage (about
   1 pound), shredded (see
   Helpful Hint)**
½ **cup chopped scallions**
1 **cup chopped pineapple**
1 **tablespoon minced
   preserved ginger**
½ **cup unsweetened
   pineapple juice**
2 **tablespoons distilled
   white vinegar**
2 **tablespoons lime juice**
1 **teaspoon salt**
1 **tablespoon vegetable oil**
½ **teaspoon freshly ground
   black pepper**

In a large bowl, mix the cabbage
with the scallions and pineapple.

In a separate bowl, mix all of
the remaining ingredients. Pour
over the cabbage mixture and mix
thoroughly. Set aside for about
30 minutes to allow flavors to
develop, or chill for a few hours
before serving.

Makes 6 servings

Helpful Hint

*Slice the cabbage with a stainless
steel knife; any other metal will
cause the cabbage to turn black.*

Per Serving:
69 Calories; 1g Protein; 3g Fat;
12g Carbohydrates; 0 Cholesterol;
397mg Sodium; 2g Fiber.

Stir-Fried Asparagus with Water Chestnuts and Peppers

2 teaspoons canola or
    vegetable oil
2 teaspoons minced fresh
    gingerroot
1 hot green or red chili pepper,
    seeded and minced
1 small red bell pepper, seeded
    and cut into ⅛-inch strips
    (about ¾ cup)
1 small green bell pepper,
    seeded and cut into ⅛-inch
    strips (about ¾ cup)
12 ounces fresh asparagus
    spears, cut into 3-inch
    pieces
½ cup vegetable broth
½ cup water chestnuts
1 teaspoon sesame oil

In a large wok or skillet, heat the oil over medium heat. Add the ginger and chili and stir-fry until fragrant, about 30 seconds. Add the green and red bell pepper strips and stir-fry for 20 seconds. Add the asparagus and stir-fry about 20 seconds more.

Add the broth, reduce the heat to medium-low and simmer, covered, until the asparagus are crisp-tender, 3 to 4 minutes. Add the water chestnuts and cook until heated through, about 20 seconds. Drizzle on the sesame oil and serve immediately.

Makes 6 servings

VARIATION

Substitute any seasonal bell peppers—yellow, purple, orange— for the red and green bell peppers.

Per Serving:
52 Calories; 2g Protein; 3g Fat;
7g Carbohydrates; 0 Cholesterol;
127mg Sodium; 3g Fiber.

Tangy Tofu Salad

Toasted, shredded nori is a traditional Japanese salad garnish.

1 cup vegetable broth

2 tablespoons soy sauce

2 tablespoons rice vinegar

1 tablespoon minced fresh
   gingerroot

2 tablespoons mirin or sweet
   white wine

1 pound firm tofu, cut into
   ¾-inch cubes

½ cup chopped scallions

One 7-inch square sheet nori

1 medium daikon radish, peeled
   and thinly sliced

In a medium saucepan, heat broth, soy sauce, vinegar, ginger, and mirin. Simmer 3 minutes. Add tofu, turning gently to coat. Simmer until tofu is lightly browned and heated through, about 5 minutes.

Remove tofu to a bowl with a slotted spoon. Increase heat to high and cook liquids until they are reduced to about ½ cup. Pour liquid over tofu. Scatter the scallions on top and let cool.

Meanwhile, toast the nori over a flame or burner, or place it under a hot broiler for a few seconds until it becomes translucent. With scissors, cut the toasted nori into ⅛ × 2-inch slivers.

Serve the salad at room temperature or chilled, surrounded by the daikon slices. Just before serving, sprinkle with nori.

Makes 4 to 6 servings

Per Serving:
126 Calories; 13g Protein; 5g Fat;
7g Carbohydrates; 0 Cholesterol;
787mg Sodium; 1g Fiber.

Malaysian Vegetable Salad in Cooked Coconut Dressing

URAP

This traditional salad boasts only humble ingredients,
but the coconut dressing gives it a rich and luxurious taste.

**3 cups finely shredded
  napa cabbage**
**1 medium cucumber, seeded
  and thinly sliced (1 cup)**
**½ large red bell pepper, cut into
  thin rings**
¼ cup coconut milk
½ cup vegetable broth
**1 small green chili pepper,
  halved and seeded**
1 large clove garlic
2 tablespoons lime juice
1 teaspoon brown sugar
1 tablespoon distilled vinegar
**1 tablespoon dried, unsweet-
  ened, shredded coconut**

Place the cabbage, cucumber, and bell pepper in a large serving bowl.

In a small saucepan, heat the coconut milk and vegetable broth to a simmer. Simmer until the mixture has reduced to ½ cup, about 5 minutes.

Mince the chili and garlic together into a paste. Add to the broth. When the broth mixture has reduced, remove the pan from the heat and cool slightly. Stir in the lime juice, sugar, and vinegar. Pour this over the salad. Set aside for 15 minutes at room temperature or chill and serve after a few hours. Just before serving, sprinkle the coconut over the top.

Makes 6 servings

Per Serving:
48 Calories; 1g Protein; 3g Fat;
6g Carbohydrates; 0 Cholesterol;
132mg Sodium; 2g Fiber.

CHAPTER 8

Desserts

Almond and Peanut Snaps

The classic Chinese restaurant almond cookie.

2 tablespoons sweet butter, softened
½ cup dark brown sugar
2 teaspoons milk or soy milk
½ teaspoon baking powder
¼ teaspoon baking soda
1 large egg, lightly beaten
¼ teaspoon almond extract
1 cup all-purpose flour
¼ cup finely chopped roasted peanuts
24 almond slivers

In a medium bowl, cream together the butter and sugar. In a separate small bowl, mix together the milk and the baking powder and soda. Add the milk mixture to the butter mixture and lightly mix in the egg and almond extract.

Add the flour and peanuts and stir until blended. Place the mixture in the freezer for 10 minutes.

Preheat the oven to 350°F.

Remove from the freezer and form the dough into a log about 12 inches long and 1 inch in diameter. Lightly oil a baking sheet or line it with a sheet of parchment paper. Cut the log into twenty-four ¼-inch rounds. Place the rounds on the baking sheet and press an almond sliver into each cookie. Bake until lightly browned around the edges, 15 to 20 minutes. Cool on a rack.

Makes 2 dozen cookies

Helpful Hint

The dough can be wrapped in plastic wrap and kept in the refrigerator for up to 1 day before baking.

Per Cookie:
60 Calories; 1g Protein; 2g Fat; 9g Carbohydrates; 12mg Cholesterol; 49mg Sodium; 0g Fiber.

Gingered Applesauce

4 large tart red or yellow apples (about 2 pounds), unpeeled, cored, and chopped into 1-inch pieces
1 tablespoon minced fresh gingerroot
1 teaspoon cinnamon
½ teaspoon nutmeg
⅔ cup mirin or sweet white wine
1 tablespoon minced crystallized ginger
2 tablespoons toasted shredded coconut

Place all of the ingredients except crystallized ginger and coconut in a medium saucepan over medium-low heat. Cover and cook 30 minutes, stirring occasionally. As the apples soften, mash them with a wooden spoon. When soft, uncover the pan and cook until all of the juices have evaporated. (The texture will be chunky.)

Transfer to a serving bowl and let cool slightly.

Meanwhile, in a small bowl or a cup, mix together the crystallized ginger and coconut and sprinkle on top of the applesauce. Serve warm, room temperature, or chilled.

Makes 6 servings

Per Serving:
120 Calories; 0g Protein; 1g Fat; 26g Carbohydrates; 0 Cholesterol; 3mg Sodium; 3g Fiber.

Star Anise Baked Apples

*Star anise is a seed pod from an evergreen tree native to China
that has a flavor similar to anise seed but slightly more bitter. It can
be found whole in most supermarkets and in Asian groceries.
This recipe takes a little longer, but it's a simple dessert
that can bake while you dine, and will be ready when you are.*

2 tablespoons honey
1 teaspoon cinnamon
½ teaspoon nutmeg
2 tablespoons apple juice
2 star anise
3 medium firm apples, halved
    and cored
2 star anise

Preheat the oven to 350°F.

In a small saucepan, bring the honey, cinnamon, nutmeg, and apple juice to a simmer. When the honey has dissolved, remove from the heat and pour into a 9-inch baking pan.

Place the apples cut-side down into the honey mixture. Spoon the mixture over the tops to coat. Pull the anise seeds apart and scatter the star "points" over the apples.

Cover the pan with foil and bake the apples until they are soft when pierced with a knife, 55 to 60 minutes. Cool slightly. Transfer the apple halves to serving plates. Strain the pan juices over the top of the apples to remove the star anise. Serve the apples warm or chilled.

Makes 6 servings

Per Serving:
60 Calories; 0g Protein; 0g Fat;
16g Carbohydrates; 0 Cholesterol;
0mg Sodium; 1g Fiber.

Steamed Banana Pudding

1 pound ripe bananas
1 large egg plus 1 large egg
   white
¼ cup coconut milk
2 tablespoons brown sugar
2 teaspoons vanilla extract
3 tablespoons rice flour
Pinch of salt
½ teaspoon cinnamon
¼ teaspoon ground cloves
Vanilla yogurt
1 tablespoon toasted shredded
   coconut

Puree the bananas in a food processor or blender, or mash by hand until fairly smooth. Transfer the mashed bananas to a large bowl and stir in the remaining ingredients except the yogurt and coconut.

Lightly oil a 2-cup shallow mold or 6 individual ¹/₃- to ¹/₂-cup molds. Spoon the batter into the mold(s).

Place the molds in a bamboo steamer. Alternatively, place an overturned bowl in the bottom of a large saucepan, pour about 2 inches of water into the saucepan, and place the molds on the overturned bowl. Cover the steamer or saucepan and steam until a cake tester inserted in the pudding comes out clean, 20 to 30 minutes. (Steaming time will vary depending on the size of the molds.) Alternatively, bake the puddings at 350°F for 25 to 30 minutes. (The texture will be slightly more "solid," more like a bread, but tasty.)

Serve the puddings warm or chilled topped with a spoonful of yogurt and a sprinkling of coconut.

Makes 6 servings

Per Serving:
134 Calories; 3g Protein; 4g Fat; 23g Carbohydrates; 35mg Cholesterol; 22mg Sodium; 2g Fiber.

Sweet Banana Rice Fritters

1 cup cooked rice
**1 medium ripe banana, thinly
    sliced (about ¾ cup)**
1 teaspoon vanilla extract
¼ cup rice flour
¼ cup all-purpose flour
¼ cup raisins
**2 tablespoons dark brown
    sugar**
¼ teaspoon ground nutmeg
¼ cup coconut milk
**2 teaspoons canola or
    vegetable oil**

In a medium bowl, mix together all of the ingredients except the oil. In a large skillet, heat 1 teaspoon of the oil. Using a ¼-cup measure, drop mounds of the batter into the hot pan. Don't crowd the pan. Cook the fritters until golden, about 2 minutes on each side. Add the remaining teaspoon of oil as needed to fry the rest of the fritters. Serve immediately.

Makes 8 fritters; 8 servings

Per Serving:
127 Calories; 2g Protein; 3g Fat; 23g Carbohydrates; 0 Cholesterol; 3mg Sodium; 1g Fiber.

Coconut Pancakes

1 cup all-purpose flour
½ teaspoon cinnamon
¼ teaspoon cardamom
1 teaspoon baking powder
1 tablespoon dark brown sugar
¼ cup coconut milk
1⅓ cups water
5 tablespoons golden raisins
1 tablespoon shredded coconut
1 tablespoon canola or
    vegetable oil

In a medium bowl, blender, or food processor, mix together the flour, cinnamon, cardamom, baking powder, and sugar. Stir in the coconut milk and water and blend until very smooth.

With a knife or in a food processor, mince together the raisins and coconut shreds and set aside.

Heat ½ teaspoon of the oil in an 8-inch nonstick skillet over medium-high heat. When the oil is almost smoking, pour in ¼ cup of the batter and tilt to coat the pan thoroughly. Cook until golden brown, about 1 minute. Flip the pancake over and cook until light brown, about 30 seconds. Remove from the pan and repeat until you have used all of the batter. (The pancakes can be kept warm in a warm oven.)

Serve the pancakes with a sprinkling of the raisin-coconut mixture.

Makes 6 servings

Per Serving:
127 Calories; 2g Protein; 3g Fat; 23g Carbohydrates; 0 Cholesterol; 3mg Sodium; 1g Fiber.

Tropical Fruit Soup

2 cups unsweetened pineapple
    juice
½ cup sweet rice wine
2 tablespoons lime juice
1 medium stalk lemon grass,
    peeled and quartered
    lengthwise
1 stick cinnamon
3 dried Thai keffir lime leaves
    (optional)
Pinch of ground cloves
¼ cup coconut milk
½ teaspoon vanilla extract
½ small fresh pineapple,
    chopped (2 cups)
1 medium ripe papaya, cubed
    (1½ cups)
1 medium ripe mango, chopped
    (1 cup)
1 medium firm banana, sliced
Mint sprigs

In a medium saucepan, bring the pineapple juice, wine, lime juice, lemon grass, cinnamon, lime leaves if desired, and cloves to a simmer. Simmer for 5 minutes; cool.

Stir in the coconut milk, vanilla, and the fruit. Transfer to a large serving bowl and chill until serving time. Before serving, remove and discard lemon grass, cinnamon stick, and lime leaves. Garnish with mint.

Makes 6 servings

Per Serving:
178 Calories; 1g Protein; 3g Fat;
34g Carbohydrates; 0 Cholesterol;
5mg Sodium; 3g Fiber.

Asian-Style Gingerbread

*This gingerbread originally was developed for the dessert menu at
Tang's Ginger Cafe in Minneapolis. It takes a little longer than
thirty minutes, but like Star Anise Baked Apples,
you can bake it while you dine.*

**3 tablespoons unsalted butter,
softened**
**2 tablespoons dark brown
sugar**
1 large egg, beaten
½ cup light molasses
**One 12-ounce can Japanese,
Chinese, or Thai beer at
room temperature**
2 cups all-purpose flour
1 teaspoon baking soda
1 teaspoon cinnamon
½ teaspoon salt
**2 tablespoons minced
crystallized ginger**
**½ teaspoon freshly ground
black pepper**

Preheat the oven to 325°F. Lightly
oil an 8×8-inch baking pan. In a
medium bowl, cream together the
butter and sugar. Stir in the egg.
Add the molasses and beer and
stir until well blended.

Stir in the remaining ingredients and pour into the prepared
pan. Bake until the cake tests done
in the center, 45 to 50 minutes.
Cool on a rack. Serve at room
temperature.

Makes 16 servings

Per Serving:
130 Calories; 2g Protein; 3g Fat;
23g Carbohydrates; 19mg Cholesterol; 185mg Sodium; 0g Fiber.

Caramelized Pineapple Rings

**1 medium ripe pineapple (about
  2 pounds), peeled, cored,
  and sliced into 6 thick rings**
3 tablespoons lime juice
1½ tablespoons honey
**2 teaspoons minced preserved
  ginger**
Mint leaves

Preheat the broiler. Place broiler rack about 6 inches from the heat source.

Place the pineapple rings on a nonstick baking sheet.

In a small bowl, mix together the lime juice, honey, and ginger to form a glaze. Brush glaze over the pineapple. Broil until the honey has melted and caramelized over the fruit, and the pineapple looks a little "charred," about 3 minutes. Garnish with mint and serve immediately.

Makes 6 servings

Per Serving:
44 Calories; 0g Protein; 0g Fat;
12g Carbohydrates; 0 Cholesterol;
1mg Sodium; 1g Fiber.

Marinated Summer Melons

1 medium stalk lemon grass, peeled
¾ cup sake or sweet white wine
1 tablespoon minced preserved ginger
2 cinnamon sticks, halved
2 tablespoons honey
2 tablespoons lime juice
About ½ honeydew melon, cut into 1½-inch chunks (2 cups)
About ½ medium cantaloupe or muskmelon, cut into 1½-inch chunks (2 cups)
2 cups chopped watermelon, cut into 1½-inch chunks

Slice the tender part of the lemon grass stalk into 3-inch pieces, then cut each piece in half lengthwise. Place in small saucepan along with the sake, ginger, cinnamon, honey, and lime juice. Bring to a boil over medium heat, then lower heat and simmer for 5 minutes. (The syrup will have turned pink and the lemon grass will have softened slightly.)

Meanwhile, combine all of the fruit in a large bowl. Remove the syrup from the heat and let cool. Pour over the fruit and stir to combine. Chill for at least ½ hour. Remove large pieces of lemon grass and cinnamon before serving.

Makes 6 generous servings

Per Serving:
119 Calories; 1g Protein; 0g Fat; 21g Carbohydrates; 0 Cholesterol; 13mg Sodium; 1g Fiber.

Oranges in Asian Mint Syrup

4 large navel oranges (about 2½ pounds)
1 tablespoon brown sugar
Zest of 1 orange, minced (about 1 tablespoon)
2 tablespoons minced crystallized ginger
¼ cup fresh lemon juice, plus more to taste
½ cup water
1 tablespoon fresh chopped mint leaves

Peel 3 of the oranges to remove skin and white pith. Set aside.

Juice the remaining orange. (You should have about ½ cup juice). Place the juice in a medium saucepan and bring to a simmer with all of the remaining ingredients except the mint. Cook for 3 minutes.

While the syrup is cooking, thinly slice the peeled oranges. Add to the pot along with any juice that collected while slicing them and heat again to a simmer. Simmer 3 minutes more.

Remove from the heat and cool slightly. Stir in the mint. Add a little more lemon juice if the oranges are too sweet. Chill before serving.

Makes 6 servings

Per Serving:
54 Calories; 1g Protein; 0g Fat; 14g Carbohydrates; 0 Cholesterol; 2mg Sodium; 2g Fiber.

Papaya Mint Salad

1 tablespoon chopped mint
2 tablespoons lime juice
Pinch of salt
2 teaspoons honey
1 tablespoon shredded coconut,
    toasted
2 tablespoons chopped roasted
    cashews
3 medium ripe papayas, halved
    and seeded
Lime wedges

In a small bowl, mix together the mint, lime juice, salt, and honey. In a separate small bowl or cup, mix the coconut and cashews. Drizzle the honey mixture into the papaya cavities. Top with the nut mixture. Serve with additional lime wedges.

Makes 6 servings

Per Serving:
51 Calories; 1g Protein; 2g Fat;
9g Carbohydrates; 0 Cholesterol;
3mg Sodium; 1g Fiber.

Plum Wine Pears

*Although yogurt isn't an authentic accompaniment
to this savory Japanese dessert, it makes a wonderful addition.*

**3 large firm Bosc pears (about
1½ pounds), peeled, halved,
and cored**
1½ cups Japanese plum wine
**2 tablespoons clover or flower
honey**
1 tablespoon lemon juice
Plain yogurt (optional)

Place the pears in a large saucepan
with the wine, honey, and lemon
juice. (The liquid will barely cover
the pears.) Cover and bring to a
simmer over medium heat. Simmer
until the pears are just tender,
20 to 25 minutes. Let cool. Serve
the pears at room temperature or
chilled with some of the liquid.
Garnish with a dollop of yogurt if
desired.

Makes 6 servings

Per Serving:
113 Calories; 0g Protein; 0g Fat;
20g Carbohydrates; 0 Cholesterol;
3mg Sodium; 2g Fiber.

Steamed Apple Pears with Sake and Mint

½ medium lemon
3 medium firm tart apple pears
    or green apples (1 pound),
    cored and quartered
1½ cups sweet sake
Zest of 1 lemon
1 mint tea bag
½ teaspoon vanilla

Rub the cut side of the lemon on each of the apple quarters. Place the sake, lemon zest, tea bag, and vanilla in the bottom of a vegetable or bamboo steamer. Place the apples in the steamer basket. Steam until a knife slips through the skin easily, 12 to 15 minutes (The apples should not be mushy). Cool slightly.

Cut each apple quarter into 4 slices and place in a bowl. Remove the tea bag from the sake mixture. There should be about 1 cup liquid. (If not, bring to a simmer and reduce to 1 cup.) Pour the sake mixture over the apples. Serve warm or chilled.

Makes 6 servings

Per Serving:
134 Calories; 1g Protein; 1g Fat;
17g Carbohydrates; 0 Cholesterol;
2mg Sodium; 2g Fiber.

Sticky Rice Bowl with Fruit

1 cup sticky rice
¼ teaspoon salt
1 ripe large mango
1 medium ripe papaya
About ½ of a ripe pineapple
¼ cup coconut milk
**2 tablespoons dark brown
   sugar**

Place the rice in a medium bowl and cover it with boiling water. Let sit for 15 minutes. Meanwhile, fill the bottom of a double boiler with water and bring to a boil.

Drain the rice and transfer it to the top of the double boiler. Add 2¼ cups boiling water and the salt. Cover the rice and cook until tender, about 25 minutes. Cool slightly.

Meanwhile, chop the mango and papaya and dice the pineapple. Add the coconut milk and sugar to the cooked rice and mix well. Transfer the rice mixture to serving bowls and top with the fruit. Rice should be served only slightly warm or at room temperature.

Makes 6 servings

Per Tablespoon:
97 Calories; 1g Protein; 3g Fat;
18g Carbohydrates; 0 Cholesterol;
101mg Sodium; 1g Fiber.

Sticky Rice and Coconut Pudding

1 quart 1% milk or plain soy milk
½ cup sticky rice, rinsed in cold water until the water runs clear (see Helpful Hint)
⅓ cup dark brown sugar
1 teaspoon cinnamon
¼ teaspoon ground cloves
1 large egg plus 1 large egg white
¼ cup coconut milk
1½ teaspoons vanilla extract
2 tablespoons shredded coconut, toasted

In a large saucepan, scald the milk. Add the rice, sugar, cinnamon, and cloves. Simmer, uncovered, until the rice is tender, about 20 minutes, stirring occasionally to prevent the rice from sticking to the bottom of the pot.

In a small bowl, beat the egg and egg white, and coconut milk with ½ cup of the hot rice mixture. Add this back to the rice pot and stir over medium heat until mixture is very thick, about 1 minute. Stir in vanilla.

Spoon the pudding into serving bowls. Serve at room temperature or chilled with a sprinkling of coconut.

Makes 6 servings

Helpful Hint

The rinsing of the rice is crucial here; without rinsing, the pudding is pasty.

Per Serving:
214 Calories; 8g Protein; 6g Fat; 32g Carbohydrates; 42mg Cholesterol; 109mg Sodium; 0g Fiber.

Sticky Rice Balls

3 cups water
Pinch of salt
1½ cups sticky rice, rinsed in
several changes of cold
water until liquid runs clear
(see Helpful Hint, page 185)
2 tablespoons brown sugar
2 tablespoons honey
¾ cup water
1 teaspoon rose water
1 tablespoon minced
crystallized ginger

In a medium saucepan, bring the water and salt to a boil. Stir in the rice, reduce the heat to a simmer, and cook, covered, until tender, 15 to 18 minutes. Remove from the heat and cool slightly.

Using a ¼- or ½-cup measure, scoop up rice mixture and form balls. Place them on a serving plate and let cool completely.

Meanwhile, in a small saucepan, heat the sugar, honey, and water to boiling. Cook until the liquid becomes a thick, bubbly syrup and is reduced to about 3 tablespoons, about 10 minutes. Remove from the heat and carefully add the rose water. Carefully spoon the hot caramel over the rice balls. The caramel should harden onto the rice balls, in a minute or so.

Makes six ½-cup balls
or twelve ¼-cup balls

Per ½ cup:
103 Calories; 1g Protein; 0g Fat;
25g Carbohydrates; 0 Cholesterol;
100mg Sodium; 0g Fiber.

Vanilla Bean Yogurt with Crispy Coconut

*The only problem with this recipe is that it is hard to wait
to eat the crispy coconut with the yogurt. Most of it is gone by
the time you're ready to assemble your dessert.*

¾ cup unsweetened coconut
   chips or shreds
2 tablespoons brown sugar
½ tablespoon minced crystallized ginger
¼ teaspoon cardamom
¼ teaspoon cinnamon
½ teaspoon vanilla extract
3 cups low-fat vanilla yogurt

In a medium wok or skillet, mix all of the ingredients except the yogurt. Turn the heat to medium-high and stir-fry until the sugar melts and the coconut browns, 3 to 4 minutes. Transfer to a plate and let cool. (The mixture will crisp up as it cools.) Spoon the yogurt into serving bowls and sprinkle 2 tablespoons of the coconut mixture over each bowl.

Makes 6 servings

Per Serving:
166 Calories; 5g Protein; 5g Fat; 27g Carbohydrates; 8mg Cholesterol; 84mg Sodium; 0g Fiber.

Roasted Bananas with Sweet Peanut Filling

**3 medium ripe bananas (about
    1 pound)**
2 tablespoons lime juice
**2 tablespoons finely chopped
    roasted unsalted peanuts**
2 teaspoons brown sugar
1 tablespoon coconut milk
½ teaspoon cinnamon
**1 tablespoon unsweetened
    coconut chips or shreds**

Preheat the oven to 350°F. Cut the bananas in half lengthwise. Brush the banana slices with the lime juice.

In a small bowl, mix together the peanuts, sugar, coconut milk, and cinnamon and sprinkle lightly over the cut sides of the banana. Then put the halves back together again. Press any remaining peanut mixture over the top and sides of the bananas. Press in the coconut.

Bake on a nonstick or lightly oiled baking sheet until the coconut is toasted and the bananas are hot, about 20 minutes. Serve the bananas immediately, cut in half or quarters.

Makes 6 servings

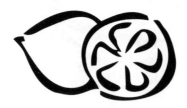

Per Serving:
87 Calories; 1g Protein; 3g Fat;
16g Carbohydrates; 0 Cholesterol;
26mg Sodium; 2g Fiber.

Mango Ice

This dessert takes a little longer because it needs to be frozen.
But it is so easy, we couldn't resist. It can easily be doubled or tripled.

**1 medium ripe mango, peeled
and sliced**
Pinch of salt
1 tablespoon honey
¼ cup water
⅓ cup pineapple juice

In a blender or food processor, blend all of the ingredients to a puree. Place it in a shallow dish and freeze until just firm, about 1 hour. Blend again and refreeze until firm. If the ice has gotten too solid to scoop, remove it from the freezer about 10 minutes before serving to soften. Just before serving, blend it again to a smooth ice.

Makes 3 servings

Per Serving:
82 Calories; 0g Protein; 0g Fat;
21g Carbohydrates; 0 Cholesterol;
2mg Sodium; 1g Fiber.

Sweet Crescents

¼ **cup chopped dried papaya**
2 tablespoons chopped peanuts
1 tablespoon brown sugar
1 teaspoon chopped
　crystallized ginger
¼ **cup raisins**
12 wonton wrappers
1 large egg white, lightly
　beaten
1 teaspoon white sesame seeds

Preheat the oven to 425°F. Place the chopped papaya, peanuts, sugar, ginger, and raisins in a food processor or blender and process to a chunky paste.

Lightly brush each wonton wrapper with water. Place 1 heaping teaspoon of papaya mixture in the center of each wrapper. Bring the ends together to form a triangle and press the edges together to seal. Place on a parchment-lined or lightly oiled baking sheet. Brush the tops with the egg white, then sprinkle with sesame seeds.

Bake until golden brown, 12 to 15 minutes. Serve warm or at room temperature.

Makes 12 crescents

Per Crescent:
52 Calories; 2g Protein; 1g Fat; 9g Carbohydrates; 1mg Cholesterol; 64mg Sodium; 0g Fiber.

Mango Crumble

1 large ripe mango, peeled and
    chopped (3 cups)
2 tablespoons lime juice
¼ cup brown sugar
6 tablespoons rice flour
½ teaspoon ground cardamom
½ teaspoon ground ginger
½ teaspoon cloves
1 tablespoon finely chopped
    macadamia nuts
2 tablespoons unsalted butter,
    softened

Preheat the oven to 375°F.

In a medium bowl, mix together the mango, lime juice, 2 tablespoons of the sugar, 2 tablespoons of the rice flour, and the cardamom. Lightly oil six ½-cup custard dishes or a 4-cup baking dish. Place ½ cup of the mango mixture in each of the custard dishes or pour all of the mixture into the baking dish.

In a separate bowl, mix together the remaining 2 tablespoons sugar, the remaining 4 tablespoons rice flour, ginger, cloves, and nuts. Using a pastry blender or your fingers, mix the butter into the mixture until crumbly. Sprinkle this over the mango mixture. Bake until lightly browned, about 25 minutes. Serve warm or at room temperature.

Makes 6 servings

Per Serving:
140 Calories; 1g Protein; 5g Fat; 23g Carbohydrates; 11mg Cholesterol; 5mg Sodium; 1g Fiber.

Roasted Banana and Pineapple Skewers

**3 medium ripe bananas
(1 pound), quartered
crosswise**
**6 large chunks fresh pineapple
(2-inch chunks about
⅓ inch thick)**
6 bamboo skewers
2 tablespoons lime juice
2 tablespoons pineapple juice
1 tablespoon honey
1 teaspoon minced fresh mint
**1 tablespoon unsweetened
coconut chips or shreds**

Preheat the oven to 450°F or preheat a barbecue grill. Thread the banana and pineapple pieces onto the skewers, beginning and ending with the banana quarters.

In a small bowl, mix together the lime and pineapple juices, honey, and mint. Brush the fruit with this mixture. If you are baking the skewers, press the coconut shreds onto the fruit. Bake the skewers on a nonstick baking sheet until the fruit is very soft and the coconut has toasted, about 15 minutes. Baste the fruit with the juices that caramelize in the pan.

Alternatively, grill the skewers over hot coals until the fruit is soft, about 5 minutes. While the skewers are grilling, toast the coconut (see Helpful Hint, page 188), and sprinkle onto the fruit before serving.

Makes 6 servings

Per Serving:
80 Calories; 1g Protein; 1g Fat; 20g Carbohydrates; 0 Cholesterol; 1mg Sodium; 1g Fiber.

Index

193

S

Hallie Harron is the executive chef of Premier Crew Restaurant Services, located in Walker, Minnesota. She has also served as a restaurant consultant to Tang's Ginger Café, a restaurant in Minneapolis serving a blend of Asian cuisines. In May 1995, she was awarded a James Beard Award nomination.

Hallie was raised in the San Francisco Bay area. Her kitchen background and education occurred primarily in Berkeley, San Francisco, and the Napa Valley. She has also had extensive restaurant training throughout France and northern Italy as well as in Indonesia and Southeast Asia.

Hallie now lives in Walker, Minnesota. She is the author/co-author of eight cookbooks and a contributor to *Vegetarian Times* magazine. Most recently she completed the ethnic noodle revision in *Joy of Cooking* (Scribner).

to learn more about
low-fat and healthy living
month after month…
SUBSCRIBE TO

❑ **8 issues $19.95** ❑ **12 issues (1 year) $29.95**

C7MFBT

**SAVE 29%
OFF THE
COVER
PRICE**

NAME _____ (PLEASE PRINT) _____

ADDRESS _____ APT. _____

CITY/STATE/ZIP _____

❑ Payment enclosed ❑ Please bill me   Offer good in US only

▲ FOR YOU

▼ FOR A FRIEND

to learn more about
low-fat and healthy living
month after month…
SUBSCRIBE TO

❑ **8 issues $19.95** ❑ **12 issues (1 year) $29.95**

C7MFBB

**SAVE 29%
OFF THE
COVER
PRICE**

NAME _____ (PLEASE PRINT) _____

ADDRESS _____ APT. _____

CITY/STATE/ZIP _____

❑ Payment enclosed ❑ Please bill me   Offer good in US only

BUSINESS REPLY MAIL
FIRST-CLASS MAIL   PERMIT NO. 106   FLAGLER BEACH FL

POSTAGE WILL BE PAID BY ADDRESSEE

PO BOX 420166
PALM COAST FL 32142-9107

NO POSTAGE
NECESSARY
IF MAILED
IN THE
UNITED STATES